THE ANALYSIS OF POWER

This book takes a new approach to the study of power by claiming that it is both necessary and possible to identify the core elements that are present in all conceivable instances of power. Unless these are properly identified, analysis is flawed, and can become fatally preoccupied with other features, such as conflict, giving information that may be important but which does not lay the necessary foundation for a thorough-going study.

As a result of looking at the approaches of writers such as Hunter, Dahl, Presthus, Agger, Goldrich and Swanson, Bachrach and Baratz, and Lukes, fifteen elements are identified as candidates, but are then reduced to the core elements: action, actor, intention and outcome. Each of these is discussed to sort out the problems presented. For example, can a collectivity be regarded as an actor, and can an exercise of power be attributed to inaction? Intention is the most troublesome, and is discussed at some length. Outcome is the most overlooked, yet is critical and leads directly into a discussion of the significance of structure.

The concept of structure has been given only limited reference in the literature on power. Where it does become the focus for debate it is immediately extended to mean structural determinism. Rejecting such an interpretation, it is argued that the concept has very definite implications concerning the positions occupied by the observer and the subject in relation to the outcome identified. The first and most basic step lies in the recognition of this essential duality. At the least, the book may be taken as a plea for realism in the study of power.

Dr. Geoffrey Debnam is Senior Lecturer in Political Science at Victoria University of Wellington, New Zealand. He worked in local government administration in England for several years before graduating from the University of Nottingham. He taught at the University of Otago, New Zealand, from 1967 to 1976, and since 1977 has been at Victoria University of Wellington, where he is currently Chairman of the School of Political Science and Public Administration. He has published articles in the *Journal of Commonwealth and Comparative Politics*, the *American Political Science Review* and elsewhere.

THE ANALYSIS OF POWER

Core Elements and Structure

Geoffrey Debnam

St. Martin's Press   New York

All rights reserved. For information, write:
St. Martin's Press, Inc., 175 Fifth Avenue, New York, NY 10010
Printed in Hong Kong
First published in the United States of America in 1984

ISBN 0-312-03284-6

Library of Congress Cataloging in Publication Data

Debnam, Geoffrey, 1931–
    The analysis of power.

    1. Power (Social sciences)   I. Title.
JC330.D4   1983   303.3'3   83-4556
ISBN 0-312-03284-6

To my wife

'between his power and thine there is no odds'

JOHNSON

Contents

Preface

Robert Dahl once likened the study of power to a bottomless swamp, and forecast darkly that we may never get through it. If I were asked to suggest an alternative, and more fanciful, title for this book, I would immediately offer *The Anatomy of a Swamp*. Its writing has been sustained by the belief that power has a few central features that should shape all exploration. These are laid out in the following pages – particularly in Chapters 2, 3 and 4. Having claimed that much, I should at once admit that any single instance of power will usually have a more complex anatomy than that exposed here. Reference to some of these other aspects can be found in the opening chapter. The swamp-like nature of power derives from the fact that these other features are never fixed. But although instances of power will differ in important ways, the core elements remain the same.

Even though the identification and analysis of these core elements are of central importance, what they then tell us about power in society dépends entirely on the way in which they are focused and structured. The concluding chapters draw attention to the nature and implications of such a claim, and to the possibility that the facts of power may exist quite independently of the observer's conceptual framework. Whoever claims to analyse power can never rely wholly on his own perceptions, however theoretically sophisticated these may be.

I would like to thank Knud Haakonsson, John Morrow, David Pearson and Bob Tristram for the help they have given me at various stages. If I have not always adopted their advice, I have nevertheless been encouraged by their interest. And although the bibliography demonstrates how wide a debt is owed for so short a work, I would like to make particular reference to Robert Agger, Robert Dahl, Daniel Goldrich, Floyd Hunter, Robert Presthus and Bert Swanson. It has been their thoughtful analyses of power in a variety of American communities that have stimulated the question that I have set out to answer here. I hope that they have no cause to regret their shared parentage. A special word of thanks is due to Keith Povey for wielding his editorial pen so discerningly in defence of the English language, and to Marion Beardsmore and Jenny Berry for making the production of typed copy such a smooth and cheerful exercise.

A version of the sections in Chapter 1 on 'Sanctions' and 'Rational Perception' appeared in the *American Political Science Review*, and I am most grateful to the editor for permission to use the material in this book.

Wellington, New Zealand   GEOFFREY DEBNAM

1 Introduction

The terms of the community power debate were set early on by confrontation between reputational and decision-making approaches. Put simply, these two approaches embodied opposed assumptions about 'power structure', and the means by which relevant evidence could be adduced. The reputational, or elitist, approach is based on the assumption that power is socially structured, and that its study must start from a statement of the nature of its structure. This view is associated with the reputational analysis techniques adopted by Floyd Hunter in his study of Atlanta, Georgia.[1] The decision-making approach denied that power is necessarily structured in the way that the elitists said it is, and argued that the only valid evidence about power had to be derived from a study of action in the decision-making arena. This view is associated with the pluralist approach of Robert Dahl.[2] A later note of radical dissent, introduced as nondecision-making, remained within this same tradition of inquiry, sharing common ground with the structural assumptions of the reputationalists, and with the methodological techniques of decision-making analysis. This third, neo-elitist, school of thought points to the diffuseness of much power operation, and argues for greater sensitivity to the problems of evidence. Originating in the work of Peter Bachrach and Morton S. Baratz, the position has been developed by Steven Lukes who rejects the exclusively behaviourist emphasis of the elitists and pluralists.[3]

The simple form of the debate has been compelling. Its particular attraction is that it has sought to combine theoretical and empirical enquiry, and in doing so has generated much valuable information about local communities. The debate has been focused exclusively, though, on the question of the location of power in society. In other words, researchers assumed that an intuitive leap into the right area would provide them with the information they required. The major problem was seen to be concerned with distinguishing the right spot on the polity's crust to start the exploration. How power was to be identified was left to the cryptically brief terms of a purportedly crucial definition.

Attempts to solve the methodological problems of power therefore have become fatally entangled with beliefs about the nature of the medium in which 'it' is located. All the major community power studies turn quite explicitly in their introduction to the theoretical aspects of power. But even where the study is most successful, as in the cases of Hunter and Dahl, it is never clear what the assembled facts owe to the introductory theory – how the spirit is made flesh.[4] The results of this eucharistic approach have been impressive but ultimately obscure. It goes without saying that the location of power is an important problem, but the argument to be developed here is that it should not be given the priority it has so far enjoyed. Because of the preoccupation with 'location', the research implications deriving from the understanding of the central concept have been overlooked. William Domhoff notes that 'Once the researcher has defined *power* to his or her satisfaction, the discussion is usually ignored in research operations'.[5] Not only is the topic ignored in research operations, it is also ignored in any conclusion based on them. Researchers do, of course, and Dahl most notably among them, turn in their conclusions to a discussion of the nature of power in society. But they do not show how their definition of power either helps them to organise their material and come to their conclusions, or stands in need of amendment. This is certainly a problem overlooked by Dahl in his study of New Haven, yet he could write seven years later that:

> The gap between the concept and operational definition is generally very great, so great, indeed, that it is not always possible to see what relation there is between the operations and the abstract definition.[6]

It is Dahl's gap between definition and operation, pointing to a feature of the community power studies that may have puzzled other readers, that is to be explored here. If, for example, we expect to find some sort of relationship between orienting definition and empirical study, we would assume that two studies showing different conclusions had either adopted different orienting definitions, or, having adopted the same, show that it can have different interpretations. Now Dahl and Hunter can certainly be shown to come to different conclusions about the operation of power. How different, though, are their orienting definitions?

HUNTER: Power is a word that will be used to describe the acts of men going about the business of moving other men to act in relation to themselves or in relation to organic or inorganic things.[7]

DAHL: A has power over B to the extent that he can get B to do something that B would not otherwise do.[8]

There are three ways in which these differ. First, Hunter locates power in an action process, whereas it can be argued that Dahl's formulation refers to a capacity. Much has been made of this distinction,[9] but it will be argued below that, while there is an obvious analytic distinction to be made between action and capacity, it collapses on closer examination. Second, Dahl makes explicit reference to the counterfactual.[10] In the absence of A's initiative, B would not have acted thus. Hunter does not make this reference, but it is difficult to imagine that he did not imply it. The third, and most obvious contrast, can be made between Dahl's limited dyadic framework, and Hunter's broader reference that seeks to capture the 'busy-ness' – his own term[11] – of life in Atlanta. The greater sense of realism shown by Hunter does not mark out a difference of principle between him and Dahl.

It is not suggested that the whole orientation of Dahl and Hunter to their subject should have been the same simply because their opening statements on power are so alike. But those statements should be significant for subsequent research in some practical way. It follows that there should be greater comparability between these studies than is the case, although this is not to say that their conclusions should have been any closer. A study of power has to be focused on some particular aspect of life, and it is this decision to select one aspect rather than another which is critical. Hunter's elitist preoccupations led him to study the activities of a few businessmen, bankers, and the like. Dahl's pluralist convictions caused him to focus on the political decision-making arena. But the focus should not obliterate the requirements of an introductory definition. The question that arises, then, is 'How should an introductory definition inform subsequent empirical study?'

This analysis does not focus exclusively on Dahl and Hunter. The other major contributions to the community power literature have also been canvassed in an attempt to establish whether their initial definitions of power show any common pattern of requirements. It could be argued, of course, that it is simply misleading to imply that anything significant can be deduced from a superficial survey of definitions. In fact, whether they are explicative definitions, operational definitions, or just simply descriptions, has not been made clear, and is often not clear in the texts from which they are taken. Of course, any attempt to express what we mean by power will be open to the criticism that an important aspect of what we understand by power has been left out[12] since there is just no agreement on what a fully comprehensive account would look like. If such an account had been sought, then a survey confined to the major community power studies would have been inadequate. On the other hand, if this restricted approach shows that the content of the various orienting definitions is identical in certain respects, can we then argue that we have identified a property, or set of properties, that is central to any description of power? This is not an essentialist argument. It is not claimed that certain elements constitute the essence of power, and that if we can state those then we have said all that is worth saying about the topic. What is asserted, however, is that certain elements may be so crucial that we ought to understand their implications before we build on any other elements that might go towards making up the variety and complexity of power situations in the real world.

Frederick Frohock points out the high mortality rate among taxonomic definitions of politics.[13] He goes on to discuss the popularity of cluster theories of reference, the logic of which require that 'no single property is essential for referential use of a term'.[14] The objective of such theories is to 'deny the traditional distinction between accidental and essential properties by denying the possibility of essential properties'.[15]

In looking at the various interpretations of cluster analysis, Frohock notes that 'cluster properties may be ranked in importance'.[16] The question therefore arises that some properties cannot be removed from referential use without impairing communication.

Language can be seen as distributed over a field whose boundary conditions are experience and whose core is resistant to change or dismissal . . . at the core of the field are statements whose retention is required for the maintenance of whole sections of the field . . . such core properties would have a fixed status for all ordinary uses of the concept; for the absence of the core properties would make the remaining cluster of properties incapable of successful reference.[17]

Frohock goes on to offer examples of fixed properties, concluding with a discussion of the centrality of reference to 'directiveness' and 'aggregation' in any account of politics. One of the features of politics, of course, that has blocked any successful taxonomic definition is its heterogeneity. The advantage of the 'core property' approach to definition is that a 'heterogeneous extension is still consistent with a homogeneous core'.[18] Core terms 'must be present for reference, but do not function to identify the event in the description'.[19] These core terms are pragmatically fixed (in the same way as the constitutive rules of chess) and are therefore essentially contestable.[20] But they can be overthrown only at the expense of the currently accepted meaning. Changing the constitutive rules of chess is always possible, but the result would not be the game of chess as it is currently known.

The question is worth asking, then; does the data that is located in 'Dahl's gap' point to a set of properties, rules, conditions, elements, or whatever, that are essential to our understanding of power? We are at the moment, of course, not asking questions about power itself, but about the sort of information that we think is necessary to understand it. This is an important qualification since an answer to the question 'is anything essential to our understanding of power?' must not be expected to be a statement about power itself. As D. M. White puts it, 'the first issue confronting anyone who would state the meaning of power is the appropriate procedure or method for doing so . . . A view of power must be devised, not the nature of power discovered'.[21]

The question will be pursued by examining the view adopted by each of six major studies in the community power debate and isolating the elements involved. This is a partial approach since only one brief orienting definition will be analysed in each case, but it is a means of access. The test will lie in the conclusions that can be derived, and in their supporting arguments. The definitions adopted by Hunter and Dahl have already been given (p. 3); those of the four other studies are as follows:

PRESTHUS: Presthus relies on Max Weber who, he says, 'defined power as the chances of "a man or group of men to realize their own will" even against opposition'.[22]

AGGER, GOLDRICH AND SWANSON: Political power is the unit attached to the outcomes of political decision-making processes and assigned to the politically participant contributors to decisional outcomes.[23]

BACHRACH AND BARATZ: Bachrach and Baratz do not formulate their own definition of power but they refer to several elements as being positively associated with power so that it is possible to construct a definition along the following lines: power can be said to have been exerted where there is a conflict of values between A and B; where A threatens B with severe sanctions in the event of B's noncompliance; where A's demand, and the severity of the sanctions, are rationally perceived by B; and where A gets his way with B's compliance.[24]

LUKES: A exercises power over B when A affects B in a manner contrary to B's interests.[25]

Each of these statements, or definitions, is seen as comprising several distinct elements that would have to be present before it could be said that the statement had been fully exemplified. For example, if Lukes' idea of power were played out before us, we would see actors acting in a certain way to produce a particular type of outcome. Itemising the requirements for such a scene would produce the list given under Lukes' name in Table 1.1. The same exercise has been performed for each of the other definitions listed. Hawk-eyed readers may well spot concepts that have been missed out. If any of these can be shown to be core elements, then the argument to be developed here would need to be supplemented; if they are not, they are irrelevant.[26]

How can we identify which of this list of concepts should be treated as core elements? Some are well subscribed. Each definition includes reference to actors and an outcome. Others are poorly subscribed. Only Bachrach and Baratz, for example, refer to compliance, rational perception, sanction and value; only Agger, Goldrich and Swanson refer to decision; and only Lukes refers to interest. Even if we dismiss these as picayune – which would be unjustified – we would still be left with nine concepts about which a small measure of agreement is shown. It is possible, however, to reduce the field by the following stratagems.

TABLE 1.1
Concepts in pursuit of power*

	Hunter	Dahl	Presthus	Agger	Bachrach	Lukes
1. Action	x			x	x	x
2. Actor	x	x	x	x	x	x
3. Affect	x	x			x	x
4. Asymmetry		x			x	x
5. Capacity		x	x			
6. Compliance					x	
7. Conflict†			x		x	x
8. Decision				x		
9. Intention	x	x	x	x	x	
10. Interest						x
11. Outcome	x	x	x	x	x	x
12. Rational perception					x	
13. Relationality	x	x			x	
14. Sanction					x	
15. Value					x	

* Two points need to be made about this table. In the first place, the fact that a particular cell has not been checked should not be taken to mean that the writer concerned dismisses that concept as irrelevant to power. The table simply represents an inventory of the contents of selected definitions. The second point to bear in mind is that we are not concerned here with interpretation. Writers may differ widely in their understanding of shared concepts, but any differences will be ignored. The problem of interpretation for selected concepts is one that will be taken up in subsequent chapters.

† Presthus' emphasis on conflict derives from a misinterpretation of Max Weber. He notes that 'Weber's emphasis upon opposition is also a critical factor; it not only sharpens the test of power, but postulates an essential condition of pluralism, namely that opposition to an elite is the best test of the existence of competing centres of power' (*Men at the Top*, pp. 4–5). By referring to Weber's emphasis upon opposition as a 'critical factor', Presthus seems to imply that Weber viewed opposition as a necessary feature of power. This interpretation is shown to be unjustified in an interesting discussion of the difficulties of translating Weber's definition from its original German form, and of the differing interpretations put upon it by leading sociologists, by Isidor Wallimann, Nicholas Tatsis and George Zito ('On Max Weber's definition of power', *Australian and New Zealand Journal of Sociology*, 13 (1977) pp. 231–5). If the power actor realises his own will within a social relationship (this last being a feature of Weber's definition that Presthus overlooks), then Weber would be prepared to recognise this as an instance of power. It may be true, as Presthus points out, that 'opposition to an elite is the best test of the existence of competing centres of power' (*Men at the Top*, p. 5). Conflict provides a ready made counterfactual. But the fact that opposition makes for an easier focal point in a study of power does not provide any theoretical justification for overriding a point central to Weber's definition – which is that neither conflict nor opposition is an essential element.

1. Some concepts must be treated as heterogeneous extensions, and not as core elements

(i) CONFLICT

That power is to be identified exclusively with instances of conflict is a matter which is contested – and this applies whether conflict is interpreted as 'conflictful behaviour', conflict of preferences, or conflict of interests.[27] Dahl's view is straightforward. 'If everyone were perfectly agreed on ends and means, no one would ever need to change the way of another. Hence no relations of influence or power would arise. Hence no political system would exist.'[28] Barry argues that 'some degree of conflict of goals is obviously a necessary condition for the exercise of power (though not the possession of power)'.[29] Nagel writes that 'most writers believe that conflict is a necessary condition of power'[30] and he cites Weber, Bierstedt, Dahl, Bachrach and Baratz, Kahn and Etzioni. The reference to Weber here is inaccurate.[31] And the view that most writers associate power and conflict is misleading.[32] If we go beyond formal declaration and look at the nature of definitions of power a very different picture emerges from that claimed by Nagel. There are, in fact, very few who refer to conflict as a necessary element and even here the reference is not always directly to conflict, but to the use of various forms of control.[33]

It is because of this association that the term 'power politics' has such pejorative overtones.[34] Interestingly, Dahl's definition of power does not fall into this category – it simply refers to changing someone else's expected behaviour. In this he is consistent with many other writers who focus on changing a respondent's behaviour without any reference to conflict, opposition or coercion.[35] As many can be sought, however, among those who define power in terms of the production of an effect, and who leave unstated whether or not conflict is involved and whether this effect might be a behavioural change.[36] A smaller number make explicit what is implicit in both these former cases – that power may involve co-operation as well as conflict.[37] Consensual power is succinctly illustrated by Collingwood. 'Watch two men moving a piano; at a certain moment one says "lift" and the other lifts.'[38] In such a situation:

> the relationship between the actors will not involve power, but a relation of power or control may exist between them jointly and

an outcome. Missing will be the threats, tension, strategy, bargaining, manipulation associated with competition for power; and attempts to apportion their joint power between them will be futile.[39]

Unless consensual power is made an explicit focus of study, the probability is that an analyst who does not specify either conflict or consensus aspects in a definition will end up by looking at conflict behaviour and events. As Nagel puts it:

> Next to power, conflict is perhaps the most frequently used term in political science; and in the other social sciences, it probably appears even more often than power. Since so much research and theorizing centers on these concepts, to explore relations between them may facilitate a useful transfer of findings.[40]

In other words, even where conflict is not part of a definition of power there is a high probability that it will become a major feature of its study (a) because it seems to be more interesting; (b) because it is more professionally rewarding, and (c) because it happens to be part of the definition of what constitutes politics (as in Dahl's reference to conflict cited above). This means that conflict will frequently figure as an important heterogeneous extension to the core elements. There is no evidence, however, that it should itself be seen as a core element.

(ii) SANCTIONS[41]

Bachrach and Baratz fail to make it clear whether or not they intend to place their several concepts on some notional 'sanctions scale', ranging from the case of manipulation (to which sanctions are held to be not relevant), through influence and authority where there are 'no severe sanctions', and power, where the 'threat of severe sanctions' applies, to the case of force which requires the actual 'application of severe sanctions'.[42] Elsewhere they imply that influence involves no sanctions at all. For example, 'the exercise of power depends upon potential sanctions, while the exercise of influences does not'.[43] In their discussion of authority no reference is made to the subject.[44]

In view of their emphasis on severity, however, it is reasonable to assume that they mean to imply a hierarchy of sanctions. But this raises the whole question of establishing an acceptable 'severity scale' against which the interpretation of the sanctions by the 'patient' in the power relationship can be measured. This is crucial to their design since severity of sanction is the only significant means of distinguishing power from authority and influence.[45]

In a later comment they say that 'sanctions are not invoked at all in situations involving authority and influence, whereas in power relationships sanctions are threatened but not invoked'.[46] There is some confusion here stemming from their apparent interpretation of 'no severe sanctions' in the case of authority to mean no sanctions of any kind. But the confusion hides no substantive point.

The difficulty created by relying on 'sanction' as an indicator of power can be briefly illustrated by citing Dahl's justification. 'Exactly what constitutes a "severe" loss or deprivation is, to be sure, somewhat arbitrary. No doubt what a person regards as severe varies a good deal with his experiences, culture, bodily conditions, and so on. Nevertheless, probably among all peoples exiled, imprisonment and death would be considered severe punishments.'[47]

This comment is so heavily qualified that it can offer no help at all to the empirical analysis of power which must deal with specific instances and, therefore, specific interpretations of the meaning of sanction as well as ways of distinguishing severe forms from others. The notion of 'severity of sanction' may be useful in comparing the power of two individuals. We may decide, for example, that if A can threaten C with death whereas B can 'only' threaten him with the loss of his job, then A would be considered more powerful. But there would seem to be no way of establishing a 'severity threshold' at which a sanction becomes evidence of power. In any event this places an unjustifiable limitation on the way we use the word 'power'. Although we continue to associate power with the ability to inflict severe sanctions, it is not a necessary association. As de Crespigny puts it, 'If it is wished to make "power" a technical term in the social sciences, it must be stripped of its dyslogistic associations. It must be used without any limitations concerning the ways in which power may be said to be exercised'.[48] To insist, then, on a necessary connection between power and severity of sanction, places an unjustifiable limitation on the way we use the word 'power'. For if A is able to get his way *without* resorting to such sanctions, it would be decidedly anomalous to say that he was, therefore, not powerful.

2. Some concepts identify the same general element

(i) Value, interest, affect, asymmetry, compliance and decision can all either be identified by, or subsumed under, outcome since any one of them can be regarded as describing the outcome of a power relationship. Each is a different way of characterising the effect of power. Whether we regard 'outcome' as the necessary test of power is another matter. Certainly, power which has no effect cannot be political power. As Dennis Wrong points out, power must produce an effect. He regards this as 'so obvious a criterion for its presence as to preclude any need for further discussion'.[49] If power does nothing, sustains nothing, and prevents nothing, then it is of no interest to the social scientist. But this raises the problem to be discussed in the next section. How can action and potential be said to identify the same body of facts?

(ii) The actual and potential facets of power are indistinguishable. Mokken and Stokman ask, is power 'a *potential* or *capacity*, or is manifest behaviour . . . the more important element? In other words should we conceptualize power and influence as *latent* or as *manifest* concepts?'[50] They propose that power 'be defined primarily in terms of potentials or capacities'[51] on the grounds that a behavioural emphasis has the unfortunate consequence of overlooking occasions such as 'when someone else does what they believe *A* wants despite *A*'s inaction',[52] more commonly referred to under Friedrich's 'rule of anticipated reactions'.[53] Barry similarly expresses preference for what Rose calls 'power as potential',[54] and supports this by appealing to the conventions of the English language.

> Power, to repeat, is not an event but a possession. The event that is associated with this possession is the exercise of power. A man has power over a period of time . . . He *exercises* power at a particular time . . . Since 'power', like 'wealth', refers to something possessed, there is no more sense in regretting the absence of a verb form than there is for regretting that there is no expression 'he wealths'.[55]

Although within any cultural setting there is likely to be a generally agreed definition of wealth, with readily available indicators to demonstrate the validity of the claim that 'wealth is a possession', we cannot speak with the same assurance for power. The English language may demonstrate certain conventional similarities in the way that we speak of 'wealth' and 'power', but this should not mask the very real differences. When we say that a man has power, we may be referring obliquely to the size of his bank balance, or to the fact that other people jump at his command; but we do not necessarily refer to anything that can be seen, or measured. In that case the only way in which power can be demonstrated is to show its relationship to some given effect.

Wealth, however, can exist without producing an effect. A man can be rich because he has inherited a fortune. If he refuses to touch the money, preferring to maintain his former life-style, that does not make him any less wealthy. But if a man in a position of power makes a decision not to use that position, either through high-mindedness, or through some groundless fears, is he still powerful? To say that he still has the power if he cares to use it is to refer to a set of circumstances which do not, in fact, exist. We are entitled to say no more than 'he could be powerful if . . .'. But that is not equivalent to the statement 'he is powerful' in the way that 'he could be wealthy if he drew his money from the bank' is equivalent to saying 'he is wealthy'. In other words, statements about power are contingent in a way that statements about wealth are not.[56]

If someone is described as powerful, then our first reaction is to ask why. The terms of the answer to this question can then be treated as the effect to be explained, although we would need to add the warning that an answer could not offer an efficient cause as an effect. For example, in asking why a politician is powerful we might be told 'because he is rich'. But such an answer would, of course, be merely tautologous, and we would need to probe further along the lines 'well, what is the effect of being rich that qualifies it to be so confidently linked with power?' The answer would identify some associated event or state of affairs as a relevant outcome, and it would be this that clarifies the claim that he is powerful. Whether the 'essential nature' of power is that it is a potential, capacity, resource, ability or behaviour is a question that is, then, regarded as beside the point. Power analysis is dependent on the identification of 'effect', or 'outcome'. It is not possible to study power in-dependently of such a notion. Once an outcome has been identified, data concerning potentiality (resources) and realisation (process) are equally valid in its analysis.

It may be difficult to disentangle potentiality and realisation in practice. Some resources emerge only in action. Polsby cites an example of 'an unprepossessive Negro dining-car waiter' who exercised power simply because he was 'extremely diligent in pressing claims on renewal planners on behalf of the welfare of his block'.[57] The resource in that case is identifiable only as a form of action. It is equally true that a resource, inert from the perspective of its owner, may be active when more broadly viewed. The individual may not choose that his resource creates a particular effect, and may do nothing to provoke it. But the effect is created. The resource is dynamic in its institutionalised setting: potentiality and realisation are indistinguishable.

What are we to conclude from this discussion? It is clear that power is too complex to be defined in terms of either resource or process characteristics unless we qualify each term to the point where both meanings merge. But while each is inadequate, neither is wholly wrong, and any empirical analysis founded on one premise will inevitably find that it has to come to terms with the facts of the other – unless myopia is taken to an extreme.

3. The reference to rational perception has no value in this context, and should be discarded

Bachrach and Baratz maintain that:

> power has a rational attribute: for it to exist, the person threatened must comprehend the alternatives which face him . . . In a situation involving power, *B* is rational in the sense that he chooses compliance instead of defiance because it seems the less of two evils. In a situation involving authority, *B* complies because he recognizes that the command is reasonable in terms of his own values; in other words, *B* defers to *A* not because he fears severe deprivations, but because his decision can be rationalized.[58]

As far as influence is concerned (the only other concept characterised by rationality), Bachrach and Baratz are less helpful. They do state explicitly that 'power and influence are alike in that each has both rational and relational attributes'.[59] But we are left to infer the nature of such rationality from the example of 'the ambitious young man who submits unhappily to the every dictate of his rich uncle . . . because he admires wealthy men'.[60]

They are arguing, then, that rationality is a sufficiently notable characteristic of these three concepts to merit particular mention. But consider the significance of what they are saying. In the case of a power relationship *B* is rational because he is dominated by fear; in the case of authority *B* enjoys the vicarious gratification of cherished values and is, therefore, rational: while rationality in their example of influence seems to mean no more than abject self-abasement. The resolution of a situation in any of these terms is held to be rational, whereas resolution by force is not because, presumably, the act of force does not depend for its success on *B*'s perception.

Notice that, in the case of power, authority, and influence, *B* is alleged to be rational because he has chosen to comply. There is an opportunity after the stimulus for *B* to behave in whichever way he wishes; but there must, by definition, be some limitation on this freedom implicit in the initial stimulus. The rationality of subsequent behaviour is, therefore, relative to the restricted definition of the situation contained in the stimulus. In the case of power, authority and influence, however, *B* has no control over the stimulus, whereas in the case of force the stimulus is, in a sense, *B*'s choice. It is *B*'s definition of the situation in as real a sense as agreement is *B*'s choice in the case of the other concepts. To deny rationality in this case, while claiming it for any emotional and submissive response, is highly tendentious. To specify subjective rationality as a condition of power raises greater problems than it may solve.

4. In the case of relationality, the problem is real enough, but it cannot be dealt with as an element of power

Bachrach and Baratz emphasise the relational aspect as a rebuttal of the view that power can be a possession.[61] But a possession can itself constitute a relationship, particularly if it represents a scarce value. If we say that someone has power, then that person is necessarily placed in a relationship with others. Relationality cannot be determined, therefore, in any crude behavioural sense. In fact, whether a relationship is held to exist may be a function of the observer's analytic framework rather than of the perception of the relevant actors. There may be disagreement, for example, as to what constitutes a scarce value. The wealthy purchaser of private medical care may reject the view that he is thereby depriving others. This is not to say that every relationship, and every valued possession, is necessarily assimilated to power. Such a judgement would have to wait upon the evidence.

The question of relationality identifies a problem of an entirely different order from those so far discussed. Any attribution of power implies a relational context within which the relevant agent is known, or anticipated, to have an effect. Just what this context is will not necessarily be known to the agent who may be quite unaware of the breadth of impact of his actions – and who may, of course, be an institution. This means that the nature, and limits, of the relational framework may have to be determined entirely by the observer. Since this structure of explanation determines what elements are identified, and what conclusions are reached, it is central to the analysis of power. Relationality is not, therefore, a core element, but identifies a problem that must be dealt with separately by looking at the relevance of the concept 'structure'.

Most of the concepts identified in Table 1.1 above are, therefore, not to be regarded as core elements. This applies to affect, asymmetry, compliance, conflict, decision, interest, rational perception, relationality, sanction and value. Capacity is also to be rejected as having such status independently. Comments made above suggest that it should be collapsed into an enlarged concept of action. From the perspective of power, capacity *is* action. Any one of the list here rejected may be useful to describe a given instance of power, but not one can be said to be necessary for all cases. There are four concepts remaining, though, that cannot be dismissed: actor, action, intention and outcome will be advanced as core elements. This means that in any conceivable instance of power that could be of interest to the social scientist, it is necessary to provide information identified by these four concepts. These are the sufficient conditions of power.[62]

2 Actors and Action

The first question to be considered is straightforward. If we say that information about actors is essential to any discussion of power, then what is to count as an actor? The approach of most contributors to the community power debate has been essentially behaviourist, emphasising the role of individuals. Agger, Goldrich and Swanson, for example, assert that 'action units are people!.[1] Although Hunter refers initially to power being structured 'into a dual relationship between governmental and economic authorities',[2] his study of Atlanta ignores the possible significance of institutional forces, concentrating exclusively on the activities of individuals. Presthus takes a similar approach, completely ignoring, for example, the role of political parties and local government. Dahl's individualist emphasis appears to be unequivocal, but, interestingly enough, much of his study of New Haven is given over to the specification of leader and sub-leader roles. This implies a degree of institutionalisation of behaviour whose implications are not, however, examined.

I

Lukes has criticised the community power studies for adopting 'too methodologically individualist a view of power'. He argues that it is essential to break with such a view because 'the power to control the agenda of politics and exclude potential issues cannot be adequately analysed unless it is seen as a function of collective forces and social arrangements'.[3] He asks whether we can attribute 'an exercise of power to collectivities, such as groups, classes or institutions', suggesting that the problem lies in identifying 'precisely how and where . . . the line [is] to be drawn between structural determination, on the one hand, and an exercise of power on the other'.[4] There are two questions here, though – what we mean by structural determination, and in what sense collectivities can be said to act. Consideration of the first will be delayed until Chapter 5, when we look at the significance in this context of the concept 'structure'. As far as the second problem is concerned, Lukes distinguishes between two forms through which 'agenda-control' power may be exerted:

> First there is the phenomenon of collective action where the policy or action of a collectivity (whether a group, e.g. a class, or an institution, e.g. a political party or an industrial corporation) is manifest, but not attributable to particular individuals' decisions or behaviour.

> Second there is the phenomenon of 'systemic' or organisational effects, where the mobilisation of bias results, as Schattschneider put it, from the form of the organisation.[5]

Bradshaw criticises Lukes for a 'holistic view of power' in which 'a political collectivity, like a party or commercial concern, may exercise power somehow independently of its leadership and body considered as individuals'.[6] Bradshaw, is not, strictly speaking, justified in drawing this as the sole conclusion. Lukes could surely claim that a policy may emerge via an incrementalist route which makes identification near impossible for outsiders, and hazardous even for members of the organisation in question. In replying to Bradshaw, though, he makes explicit his reliance on an essentially behavioural position, but one which is heavily modified by the need to emphasise role-playing within a specific, and complex, organisational space. He argues that although institutional power is 'exercised by virtue of what these component individuals do, or do not do . . . it cannot be reduced to or identified with or exclusively explained by their behaviour or their decisions'.[7]

Lukes is not suggesting that power may be exercised, identified and discussed in the absence of action by individual actors, but that 'actions and inactions cannot be identified, let alone explained, without reference to a whole vast network of cultural, social and institutional factors'.[8] Bradshaw would, no doubt, make exactly the same stipulation. Jessop notes that 'insisting on the complex relations between individual action and social constraints . . . is not a solution to the problem'[9] which Lukes himself had identified as escaping from the methodological individualism of earlier approaches. In fact, as several critics point out, not only does Lukes' three-dimensional approach *not* offer a solution, it ends up by retreating to the same base in methodological individualism that it sought to demolish.[10] Part of the confusion, it is suggested, has arisen because the two questions of structural determinism, and of collectivity as actor, have not been separated. It may be possible to say that collectivities can be seen as actors without accepting that as evidence of structural determinism. How, then, can a collectivity be said to exercise power independently of its members? There are at least three possible avenues to explore.

(i) COLLECTIVITY AS IMAGE

A collectivity can be said to exercise power where it develops a corporate identity that acts as a motive on the minds of others. Party images, for example, have long been recognised as important in sustaining voting support.[11] Max Weber argued the point as follows:

> These concepts of collective entities which are found both in common sense and in juristic and other technical forms of thought, have a meaning in the minds of individual persons, partly as of something actually existing, partly as something with normative authority . . . Actors thus in part orient their action to them, and in this role such ideas have a powerful, often a decisive, causal influence on the course of action of real individuals.[12]

Although we have to explain the existence of such ideas by reference to the intended and unintended consequences of individual action, these 'concepts of collective entities' do exist and are interpreted by others as representing an intention or purpose to which they respond accordingly. In explaining these responses it would be quite unnecessary to consider the origin of the image. We do not need to know about the activities of individual members to understand any such claim. We do not need to explain how the image came about, just as we do not need to know how an explosive was made to appreciate its devastation. In this sense, then, the collectivity *qua* image is power and can be said to exercise power so long as the case meets whatever other conditions we associate with power. That assertion cannot be refuted by noting that such power can be traced to the actions of individuals.

(ii) COLLECTIVITY AS ACTOR

The second way in which a collectivity may be said to exercise power would involve a defence of holism. For example, one would have to accept that there is a real sense in which the actions of an army cannot be reduced to the actions of the soldiers comprising it. Jarvie would deny this, insisting that ' "Army" is merely a plural of soldier and *all* statements about the Army can be reduced to statements about the particular soldiers comprising the Army'.[13] Lukes argues that 'this theory is only plausible on a crude verificationist theory of meaning'.[14]

It can be argued, of course, that a verificationist theory of meaning might be crude, but still remain useful. As an alternative to saying that the green army beat the blue army, we could, if we had all the data, lay out a series of individual actions that would explain what the simple statement of victory could not. Most of what we explain by reference to 'army' can be dealt with by microscopic analysis. The result is, of course, tedious – as anyone reading the battle scenes in *The Iliad* can attest. Collective concepts relieve us of the tedium of that sort of description. In practice, we can seldom be aware of all the relevant individual contributions when we move beyond a certain size and number. We have to act in some respects as if 'army' is the primary explanatory concept. But such a tactic is acceptable only where the detailed evidence is lacking – which is why war historians spend so much energy trying to determine precisely what this troop or that platoon was doing at a certain time. What from a distance might be understood as the power of the army can, from a closer view, be attributed to its proper source.

Jarvie is right to demand verification – crude or not, it is necessary. But Lukes is also right to be suspicious of the implications of Jarvie's claim. Sometimes verification can go only so far. Where the image of the collectivity acts on the minds of others, there is small profit to be gained from trying to take the image apart. For example, suppose that we wanted to understand the outcome of an encounter where the blue army ran away on hearing that the green army was advancing. The statement concerning the blue army would have to be reduced to statements about soldiers before it had any significant meaning. But the effect of the green army could not be attributable to the actions of any of its individual parts, who would be irrelevant to any explanation (for example, that the blue army soldiers had no weapons, or were all cowards).

The unwelcome effect of Jarvie's argument, if accepted in the extreme form in which he poses it, would be to lead to a retreat from holism into methodological individualism. This theory, as Lukes explains, holds that 'no purported explanations of social (or individual) phenomena are to count as explanations . . . unless they are couched wholly in terms of facts about "individuals" '.[15] But we have seen in the foregoing example that we would add no more to the explanation of the green army's victory by any statements about green army soldiers. It is true that we have to note the relevant information about the soldiers of the opposing army, but that does not discount the fact that the green army remains an irreduceable concept in this case.

Both Joseph Agassi and J. O. Wisdom[16] have shown how Karl Popper offers 'institutional' or 'situational' as an alternative to 'methodological' individualism. This Popperian approach denies that groups can have intentions or purposes independently of their members, but accepts that, for the purposes of socio-political explanation, individuals must be identified in an institutional setting. For example, explanation of a political party's victory at a general election may be made by reference to the actions of various individuals in their party capacities. The fact that the party is the basic explanatory unit does not give it an existence independent of those members. Nor can we point to the legacy of previous generations as having such status. Of course, present members will be affected by such a legacy, but that, in its turn, may be similarly reducible to the actions of individuals. Any point of focus may be explained in this way – the way that Jarvie wants – but the process of focusing necessarily means that we must then consider the world from the point of view of the individuals so isolated. This will involve accepting the same institutional reference points which motivated those individuals. For example, the party member will be oriented towards other parties, the electoral system, the legislature, and so on. In explaining that party member's behaviour, we cannot reduce those institutions without distorting the behavioural stimulus. This means that explanation can never be entirely reduced to statements about individuals, since that would misrepresent the world inhabited by our actors. As Wisdom puts it, 'you can dispense with one or even more institutional wholes, *but only in an institutional setting*'.[17]

This reinforces the conclusion of the previous section concerning the significance of collectivities as images in the minds of individual actors. The image is the external aspect of a collectivity. Its nature will ultimately depend on the collectivity's internal structure,[18] but on any given occasion it can itself be the efficient cause of action by others. A collectivity cannot respond to stimuli as an individual does, but it can be regarded as an active force, causing others to act in ways that are congenial to its continuity.

(iii) COLLECTIVITY AS RULES

A third possible example of a collectivity exercising power independently of its individual members occurs where the collectivity's rules produce effects that do not necessarily, in any given instance, represent what those members might have decided if they had approached that as a fresh problem. This coincides with Lukes' second source of 'agenda-control' power. But to attribute power to the collectivity *qua* rules is to ignore the significance of the figures behind the rules.

This does not entirely dispose of the problem because we might want to refer to an occasion where the formal or informal rules, or any other aspect of the collectivity, created an entirely unforeseeable, and even unwelcome, outcome. Both Hayek and Popper would place unintended effects at the head of the agenda for the social sciences.[19] The sense in which unintended effects could be central to a study of power is not clear, however, particularly if intentionality is regarded as a crucial feature.[20] Further discussion should wait upon a better understanding of what we mean when we talk about intentions. This will be attempted in the next chapter. For the present, though, this third area does not appear to yield any sense in which a collectivity can be said to exercise power independently of its members.

The only way in which we are justified in going beyond the individual in identifying power actors is where we can establish that the image of a collectivity acts as a motive in the minds of individuals. Collective images of this sort can be unpacked if necessary so that the individuals responsible for the image can be identified, but it is not those individuals that the affected others respond to. In such a case we are justified in identifying a collectivity as an actor, but in no other. It goes without saying that an approach that accepts intangibles as actors cannot rely on the unaided perception of the observer. The only way in which this information can be available to the researcher is by asking those apparently involved.

II

An approach that is prepared to recognise the possibility that collectivities can be treated as actors in the sense outlined above does not sit well with the understanding of action that is predominant in the community power literature. In most cases the emphasis is on action as decision-making. This is as true for Hunter as it is for Dahl. Despite being associated with a structural approach, Hunter is equally preoccupied with action related to decision-making.[21] Agger, Goldrich and Swanson are also concerned with the political decision-making process which they break up into various stages. In practice these do not open up anything not already available through Dahl's approach – they simply systematise. But an apparently casual comment raises a point that is worth pursuing. They note that the stage they call policy formulation 'occurs when someone *thinks* that a problem can be alleviated, solved or prevented by a shift in the scope of government'.[22] This reference to 'thinking' calls for further comment. In what sense can we accept thought as an action? Surely there is a fundamental distinction to be drawn between the two which is so significant that the authors would have been expected to argue the point if they had intended it. Perhaps we should, then, ignore this and assume that when they talk of action they refer to the various overt movements that any casual (but conveniently placed) observer could interpret as an outward sign of socially meaningful orientation. Yet our problem lies not so much in accepting the distinction between thought and action, as in deciding whether the consequences of thought are to be regarded as actions only when accompanied by 'overt movements' of some sort.

Agger, Goldrich and Swanson do refer to the possibility of this 'thinking' stage *not* leading on to the following stage of policy deliberation. In this case the political decision-making process 'has been started but is stillborn'.[23] Suppose that these two events or conditions, (a) formulation of preference, and (b) no policy deliberation, can be linked to a third event or condition, i.e. (c) decision-making outcome. It is, after all, very easy to imagine a train of events that, as all participants are aware, depends on the intervention of a particular actor at a crucial stage. If an alternative outcome can be attributed to lack of apparent action by that actor, would we then want to say that the outcome should be attributed to 'pure thought'; or that the actor therefore becomes a null factor and cannot be said to have contributed to the outcome?

To take an example from John Stuart Mill: consider the case of a man about to cross a bridge which a bystander knows to be unsafe. Mill uses the example to debate whether being forcibly restrained from crossing under such circumstances could be said to constitute a limitation on liberty. Mill asserts that such a conclusion would be unreasonable since 'liberty consists in doing what one desires, and he does not desire to fall into the river'.[24] Knowing this, the bystander would be responsible for any harm that follows, and in this context 'responsible' must be taken to mean 'being the cause of an action'.[25] We would say that, in this example, the bystander has the power to harm, and the power to avoid harm. Both of these have equal status as possible events. If we were to observe the pedestrian about to cross the bridge, with the bystander close enough to be heard by the pedestrian and to stop him forcibly if necessary; if we knew the condition of the bridge, and that this information was known to the bystander, but not to the pedestrian; and if we knew nothing at all about the state of mind of the two parties: then future events would be entirely contingent. We would say that the bystander had two choices of action open to him: to prevent, or not to prevent. Each outcome can be explained by reference to a decision *plus whatever is necessary to put that decision into effect.* In other words, it is the 'post-decision executive procedure' that constitutes action, and this is true even if it displays no physical properties. Agger, Goldrich and Swanson do not draw this sort of conclusion from their example. They are preoccupied with 'actions that were part of actual decision-making processes', and in such a way that overt forms are emphasised. They recognised that less obvious forms of political action might be relevant to a study of power, but admit that 'when the significance of non-decision-making politics was realised, it was too late to extend the research focus appropriately'.[26]

Bachrach and Baratz have, however, tried to develop this concept of nondecision-making into a central position in the study of power. How does this add to our understanding of the variety of forms of political action? Although they label nondecision-making succinctly as 'a decision that results in suppression or thwarting of a latent or manifest challenge to the values or interests of the decision-maker',[27] their further discussion of its nature points to two separate types of process that may be called 'covert control' and 'mobilisation of bias'.

Covert control offers nothing new. One form occurs when the

action is hidden from the relevant public. Bachrach and Baratz cite various forms of force, including 'harassment, imprisonment, beatings and even murder'[28] although, as Parry and Morriss point out, imprisonment is in rather a different category from the others – at least, if legal imprisonment is meant.[29] In these cases the politician intends that the action should be hidden, no doubt because it is so transparent that the motive could not otherwise be masked. The second variant occurs where the politicians' action is public, but where the purpose is effectively hidden. Bachrach and Baratz point to any means that 'invoke an existing bias of the system – a norm, precedent, rule or procedure'.[30] It does not necessarily follow, of course, that this form has to be exercised covertly. But even where the action itself is open, the intention will be masked. Neither of these covert forms adds anything to the vocabulary of political action as elaborated by Hunter, Dahl, or any other student of community power.

Bachrach and Baratz can be interpreted to mean that mobilisation of bias is a second form of nondecision-making. This is the area in which their writing is most potentially innovative. But it is also the area in which they have most changed their position as a result of criticism. If at any point in the debate their preoccupation with mobilisation of bias can be shown to have substance, then this could well represent an advance in our thinking about the nature of relevant action.

Mobilisation of bias refers to Schattschneider's oft-quoted formulation that 'all forms of political organization have a bias in favor of the exploitation of some kinds of conflicts and the suppression of others because *organization is the mobilization of bias*'.[31] The difficulty presented by Bachrach and Baratz's writing is that 'mobilisation of bias' can either be construed as the explanation, the cause, of issues being kept out of the public arena, or as relevant only in so far as it is manipulated for that purpose by an actor. This second view is put forcibly by them in refuting the first interpretation:

> In very plain language, we said [*Power and Poverty*, p. 44], 'The primary method for sustaining a given mobilization of bias is nondecision-making.' We went on, there and subsequently, to distinguish carefully between those who exercise power to create, shape or reinforce the mobilization of bias and the mobilization of bias itself, secure in the understanding that failure to make the distinction could lead to the error of focusing solely upon the

mobilization of bias to the exclusion of actors who exercise power and its correlates to sustain the mobilization and make it politically effective.[32]

But the earlier writings of Bachrach and Baratz can be cited in support of the more radical interpretation that assigns an apparently independent role to the mobilisation of bias:

> When the dominant values, the accepted rules of the game . . . singly or in combination, effectively prevent certain grievances from developing into full-fledged issues which call for decisions, it can be said that a nondecision-making situation exists . . . the mere existence of the 'mobilization of bias', to use Schattschneider's phrase, is sufficient to prevent a latent issue from becoming a question for decision.[33]

And in their reply to the criticism of Richard Merelman, they wrote that the nondecision-making process:

> is at work when the mobilization of bias, created or sustained by its beneficiaries (who may be either elites or non-elites), is *sufficiently dominant* – not necessarily or even usually omnipotent and all encompassing, as Merelman contends – to prevent a political issue from reaching the decision-making arena.[34]

These statements are unequivocal. However much political actors may wield power through using the mobilisation of bias, it must itself be regarded as powerful if action and inaction can be attributed directly to it without any other mechanism intervening. Consider the example brought forward by Bachrach and Baratz of the academic at a meeting where he had intended to voice critical views.[35] When his turn comes to speak he sits mute, inhibited from saying anything by his estimation of the likely reception and its consequences. Here, it seems, is a case where the academic recognises a barrier to the public airing of conflict, and defers to it. There is a strong temptation, therefore, to infer from this that the example illustrates some form of power. But as there is no apparent interaction we would have to describe this as 'action at a distance' which certainly does not accord with the pluralist's view of power.[36]

Such an example provides scant evidence for saying that the mobilisation of bias is therefore a form of action. Bachrach and

Baratz affirm such an attribution in the two quotations cited above, but then supply a causal view of power whose implication leads to the rejection of such a role being assigned to the mobilisation of bias. They took the latter course, and in *Power and Poverty* the mobilisation of bias is referred to simply as a tool to be used by actors in the pursuit of their objectives. It is put forward there as operating only through the agency of initiating actors.

Having disposed of the aspect of their argument that conflicted with their causal view of power they then modified this interpretation under further challenge. They first removed the requirement that there should be clear communication between the two sides of a power relationship. They argued that 'it often happens that neither *A* nor *B* is aware of the other's existence, yet one can exercise power over the other'.[37] But the greater the distance between *A* and *B*, the more difficult it is to isolate *A* as the necessary and sufficient factor in *B*'s response, which is what they take to be the defining characteristic of a causal interpretation. They therefore propose an alternative. 'A more useful formulation of power is one which states that a person or group exercises power to the extent that he, she or it *contributes* to shaping or strengthening barriers to public airing of grievances'.[38] Having abandoned their initial position on power, though, they must recognise that it leaves them with no defence against the re-adoption of their original interpretation of mobilisation of bias. Once the direct link between *A* and *B* is broken, there is no way of restricting the number of intervening links. Bachrach and Baratz offer no means to structure such an indeterminate linkage, although they claim to be preoccupied with the question, 'How can one be certain in any situation that the "unmeasurable elements" are inconsequential, are not of decisive importance?'.[39] Their own research techniques are superficial, and compare unfavourably with the studies they are designed to supplant.[40]

Thus far two separate issues have been raised touching on the nature of action. The first concerns the status of inaction in the power debate. In what sense can we legitimately view an exercise of power as deriving from inactivity? And does it make any difference if this exercise is conscious or unconscious? The second question concerns the possibility that a mobilisation of bias, or some other similar agency, can be regarded as a power actor. Bachrach and Baratz's discussion of this area has been shown to be inadequate, but the question is worth re-phrasing in a rather more specific form.

Steven Lukes has considered the question of power through

inaction. He focuses his discussion on the work of Matthew Crenson who seeks to explain why towns with comparable air pollution levels failed to act at the same time to deal with the problem. In the particular case of Gary, Indiana, Crenson suggests that 'in spite of its political passivity US Steel seems to have had the ability to enforce inaction on the dirty air issue'.[41]

Apart from showing that Gary moved at a slower pace than the neighbouring city of East Chicago, Crenson offers no evidence in support of this claim. Far from there being a satisfactory non-behavioural explanation of this 'outcome', it seems that there is a perfectly adequate behavioural one. We need only take account of the salience and connections of 'Chris Angelidis, a sanitary engineer employed in the city Health Department, who asked permission to write an air pollution ordinance for Gary'.[42] Crenson ignores that Angelidis had been employed in pollution control work by neighbouring East Chicago's Inland Steel Company.[43] The fact that the ordinance 'that he saw fit to write . . . was in large measure tailored to the interests of US Steel'[44] need not then be interpreted in the way that Crenson does. When we understand that Angelidis was probably simply repeating lessons that he had learnt with East Chicago's Inland Steel Company we have to take a different view of US Steel's significance. It was not that company's inaction that created any particular outcome. And the fact that US Steel may have benefited from Angelidis' predilections cannot be taken as evidence that the company had any power in the matter – apart from the power to drag its heels.

A similar objection can be made against John Gaventa's claim[45] that the American Association Ltd exerted power over the people of Clear Fork Valley without requiring any form of overt action. It is true that the Association appeared to be aloof from events in the valley. But the relationship is a complex one, as Gaventa recognises. He draws attention to the following quotation from the *Guardian*:

> If seven men with computers studied the Lowson empire for half a year they would probably not disentangle the network . . . It is like a gigantic molecule whose characteristics depend not just upon its general shape but on the precise relationship of one part with another.[46]

From the point of view of this discussion the conclusion is that much of what is attributed to inaction in this corporate context is quite possibly to be explained by unfamiliarity with devious modes of action.[47] It is worth also pointing out, though, that we should not expect the initiating action and its appropriate responses to be proximate in time. A successful teacher may be the cause of behaviour years after the lesson was preached.[48] It would be inaccurate, though, to say that the behaviour could be attributed to the teacher's inaction. We would have to explain the behaviour by reference to the teacher's action years before. It is unrealistic to carve time into chunks that separate initiating action from effect, and then argue that because of this separation we have to explain the effect by reference to spooks.

This discussion is not intended to dismiss the relevance, or significance, of inaction in a study of power, but merely to suggest that no satisfactory study of it, at least within the context of the power debate, has been developed. Yet it must surely be uncontentious to claim that an actor's failure to act on certain occasions may be read as the cue for action or, as Lukes points out,[49] inaction by others – and that such a relationship could meet any other criteria considered necessary for power. Lukes does not discuss this at any length and simply makes two brief points. The first is relatively trivial and concerns his reference to inaction as a 'non-event'. Of course, what he means is fairly clear. Inactivity has no outward behavioural manifestation and in that sense is not a physically proclaimed event. But quite obviously when something does not happen that everyone expects to happen then they are entitled to regard that as an event in every sense of the word. Lukes goes as far as to say that inaction is not 'a featureless non-event'.[50] I would go further and suggest that socially oriented inaction is most decidedly an event. The term 'non-event' is misleading and should be rejected in this context.

Ball demonstrates something of the confusion that surrounds this term. He describes events as 'occurrences, happenings, overt behaviour'[51] and notes that 'dispositions, attitudes, standing conditions, processes, etc.'[52] are non-events. He correctly argues that these can be causes just as much as occurrences, happenings and overt behaviour. He misses the point though that, in the case of overt behaviour, it is not the behaviour itself which constitutes the event, but its recognition as having the status. The politician declaiming before the mirror does not constitute an event. This is truly a non-event if no one notices and no one is affected. Its status as event is not determined by the particular sequence of actions which have to be gone through for a politician to speak, but by the recognition by whoever is affected, or notices. Merelman argues that 'non-*Events* are, by definition, non empirical. You cannot observe what has not happened'.[53] Perhaps the best illustration of the inaccuracy of this comment – which Ball describes as 'a metaphysical howler' comes from Conan Doyle's story 'The Adventure of Silver Blaze':

> 'Is there any other point to which you would wish to draw my
>   attention?'
> 'To the curious incident of the dog in the night-time.'
> 'The dog did nothing in the night-time.'
> 'That was the curious incident,' remarked Sherlock Holmes.

How did Sherlock Holmes recognise this incident? By employing what his contemporary, Max Weber, describes as an 'organic approach', Holmes recognised the field of relevant actors, and was able to predict their probable response to a given event. Where the actual behaviour differed, it constituted an event to be explained – even though it had no physical manifestation. To revert to Weber's terms, Sherlock Holmes sought 'to understand social interaction by using as a point of departure the "whole" within which the individual acts'. Weber goes on to point out that 'in certain circumstances this [functional frame of reference] is the only available way of determining just what processes of social action it is important to understand in order to explain a given phenomenon'.[54]

In the majority of cases cited so far – Mill's bystander, US Steel and Sherlock Holmes' dog – the assumption has been that inaction was a conscious choice. There is no difficulty in assimilating such examples to the hagiography of power. But what of the case where action is unconscious? Can we possibly accept an unconscious action as an exercise of power? Lukes notes three different ways in which one can be said to exercise power unconsciously. One may be unaware of (i) 'what is held to be the "real" motive or meaning of one's action (as in standard Freudian cases)'; (ii) 'how others interpret one's action'; or (iii) 'the consequences of one's action'.[55] Bradshaw describes these three aspects of an interaction as 'cause, reception and result'.[56] He wishes to distinguish ignorance of any of these from ignorance of the entire process where, of course, the power actor would be unaware of all three aspects. Such a possibility occurs in the case of anticipated reactions, where *B* responds to what he takes to be *A*'s wishes without their conscious promotion by *A*. Is this unconscious action? This more general case will be returned to when each of Lukes' three categories has been examined to determine in what sense a power actor might be unconscious of *aspects* of the power process and yet still be described as powerful in relation to it.

(a) *Must the powerful be self-aware?* In relation to the first 'Freudian case' Lukes argues as follows:

> Identifying an unconscious exercise of power of the first type presents the usual difficulty, characteristic of Freudian-type explanations, of establishing the real motive or meaning, where the interpretation of observer and observed differ. This difficulty, however, is well-known and has been very widely discussed, and it is not peculiar to the analysis of power.[57]

Let us suppose, for the sake of simplicity and to fit in with Lukes' ideas, that an act of power consists of *A* intentionally harming *B*'s interests. The 'Freudian case' would comprise one of two possibilities. *A* might consciously intend to harm *B*'s interests, and do so despite being unaware of his 'real' motives. This creates no difficulties for power analysis and conforms to Lukes' idea of power. Most of us, for much of the time, may be partly or wholly wrong in our interpretation of our motives for action. Confusion over motivation, however, need not obliterate our consciousness of what it is we are doing. Suppose that actor *A* intends to affect actor *B* in a certain way, and does so. In what way would we want to qualify the conclusion that *A* had exerted power over *B* if we were told 'but *A* didn't do that for the reasons he admitted to – he was really motivated by some other consideration'?

Alternatively, *A* might not consciously have intended to harm *B*, but nevertheless did so in accordance with his subconscious motivation. In this case, the observer would spot the discrepancy between stated intention and subsequent action, and would have to make one of two assumptions:

1. either the action did, in fact, embody *A*'s real intentions, leaving open as irrelevant the reason for discrepancy
2. or *A* was plainly stupid, or ill-judged, in choosing a course of action that was in conflict with his intentions.

If the observer has good reason for making the first assumption he would conclude that the example fits Lukes' definition of power. The problem arises in distinguishing such a case from the alternative. If, for example, *A* wanted to help *B*'s chances of election to the party leadership, he might decide to speak in his favour at a party meeting. However, he does not recognise the general hostility to his own person – a hostility that is displaced, to a greater or lesser extent, onto everything he supports. His speech has the inevitable effect of losing votes for *B*, who fails in his leadership bid. The problem here, though, is not one of the agent's unawareness of what he intended, but of his failure to recognise how his acts were interpreted. The cases arising under Lukes' first category of the unconscious exercise of power – the 'standard Freudian case' – either present, as he suggests, no special problem for power analysis, or else collapse entirely into his next category.

(b) *Must the powerful be understood?* In the second example Lukes asks how *A* can exercise power over *B* if *A* is unaware of how *B* interprets his actions. Lukes dismisses consideration of this by saying that 'identifying an unconscious exercise of power of the second type seems to pose no particular problem'.[58] But it is as well to make explicit what is involved here. If others mistake the meaning of a particular action, and respond to their own misconceived notion rather than to the agent's intended meaning, then we have to ask (1) what it was that caused the misperception in the first place; (2) what it was that resulted in the substitution of some other meaning; (3) why the others responded to this substituted meaning in the way they did; and (4) how the substituted meaning related to the agent's values. Each of these will be looked at in turn.

(1) It would seem inappropriate to describe someone as powerful who is just unable to get others to understand the nature of his action. We would be even more reluctant in the case where the substituted meaning runs counter to the agent's intention. It might be argued, though, that even where the agent is unable to control the interpretation of his actions, so that the outcome works against his interests, the agent must, nevertheless, be regarded as the cause of what follows and as powerful on that count alone. But here we must ask the second question posed above.

(2) What was it that made the others identify that particular interpretation of action? The range of possibilities can be presented as a continuum. At one extreme the answer can be posed as some attribute which is highly specific to *A*, in the sense that it is created

by him and owes little to other agencies for its force. Charismatic authority would be an example, possibly. Further along the continuum the answer could be sought in attributes which are not specific to A, in the sense that their force properly derives from some other source, but which happen to be currently available to A. This would include the force that derives from formal position. Then it is possible that others would interpret A's words or actions wrongly, not because they are misinterpreting an attribute of A's, but because of something which is in the context of that action. Circumstances may fortuitously lend urgency to the most modest request, and may also confuse its meaning. Finally, the misinterpretation may arise entirely out of B's preconceptions of what would be expected of him in such a situation, or genuine confusion over meaning.

(3) In answering the question 'why did B respond to this substituted meaning in the way that he did? ', it is fairly clear that A could be advanced as the reason in only the first extreme case. Here the 'force' that B mistakenly responds to is A's. If we can describe that force as power then clearly we are talking about A's power. Where B responds to the position that A occupies, however, it would be misleading to talk of that as if it were A's power in the same way as in the first example. The position is, of course, A's position. But it is no more his power than the rented or tied house is the tenant's. B would be responding to the position, and not to A. We could only understand the nature of power in this case by understanding the nature of the position and B's relation to it. In the next case where A's action is performed in a distorting context, the answer to B's response must be sought in the nature of that context and not in any attribute or connection of A's. Similarly, where B's misinterpretation cannot be explained by reference to either A's personal or official attributes, but only by reference to some entirely egocentric confusion it would be foolish to attempt any explanation of B's subsequent behaviour by reference to A's power. It is the nature of B's interpretation in these various cases, then, that allows us to decide whether the power factor can be said to be A's; whether it belongs to a position he occupies; is accounted for by some feature of the situational context; or simply reflects some private fantasy of B.

(4) If the substituted meaning is hostile to A's values, then we may describe the outcome as evidence of power only if we use the notion of negative power. Dahl has made such a suggestion,[59] which has been rejected by de Crespigny, who points out that 'failure to

exercise power is not exercising negative power; it is not exercising power at all'.[60]

Our initial conclusion must be that the powerful need not always be understood. If others respond (even if mistakenly) to the resources or attributes of the powerful, then that constitutes an unconscious exercise of their power. But in most cases the response would be attributable to the institutionalisation of that resource (e.g. wealth) rather than to characteristics uniquely associated with one actor. The reputedly powerful may be captives of the institution they use. Misunderstanding can therefore point to the power of the institution in the minds of others, and to the inability of the reputedly powerful to control it.

(c) *Must the powerful know the effect they cause?* The third possible instance of the unconscious exercise of power occurs where A is unaware of the consequences of his action. Lukes suggests that where A could have taken steps to find out what these were likely to be (i.e. where the relevant information was available), it is relevant to describe the consequences as an exercise of A's power. Conversely, where A could not possibly have known what the effect of his actions was likely to be, then that effect cannot be taken as evidence of his power. Cigarette companies, Lukes argues, did not exercise power over their customers before information was available to suggest that smoking could be harmful. Where they could reasonably have discovered those consequences, he believes that their decision to continue selling a commodity that could kill was an exercise of power.[61]

Consider, however, what it means to say that they 'could, in the context, have ascertained those consequences'. It could either mean that they suspected that there might be some harmful consequence, but chose not to find out. Alternatively, they might have known that they were not acting according to accepted definitions of their role. This latter possibility does not require that they suspect that any harm derives from their actions, but simply that they have not carried out the precautions expected of a cigarette manufacturer in that context. In these two cases, the manufacturers are conscious, albeit in a diminished sense, of action that could be harmful. In both cases their power is as real as the power of Mill's bystander in exercising the option of not restraining the endangered pedestrian.

Even if the cigarette companies were not aware in any given case that a particular person had contracted lung cancer through smoking cigarettes which they (and not another manufacturer) had produced, they would still understand the statistical probability that any one smoker might be harmed in that way. Power actors need not necessarily be aware of the detailed consequences of their actions. In answer to the question 'must the powerful know what effect they have caused?', we have to reply 'yes!'. But such an answer must immediately be qualified by adding that the awareness may be indirect and generalised.

This argument has so far considered the case where the power actor is possibly unaware of some aspect – cause, reception or result – of the power process. It remains to consider the problem from a broader perspective in which the power actor remains unaware of the process as a whole – where the power subject anticipates the likely reactions of the power holder and tailors his response accordingly. The topic has been well argued by de Crespigny, who cites the following example from Dahl and Lindblom. 'The boss who comes to work in a grumpy mood may not intend to induce his secretary to treat him gently; yet the responses of a good secretary are as definitely controlled as if the boss had deliberately asked her to smooth the way a little more than usual that day.' He goes on to argue that:

> the boss does intend that his secretary should treat him gently. It is true that on this occasion he does not deliberately get her to act in this way, and may be unaware of the special treatment he is receiving, but nevertheless her conduct does accord with his intentions. For it may be assumed that those who employ secretaries possess intentions that cover this kind of behaviour.[62]

It seems that the secretary occupies roughly the same position as Bachrach and Baratz's mute professor. Have we, therefore, simply arrived back in the obscurities of the mobilisation of bias? Why should norms of courtesy recognised by the secretary be regarded as the operation of boss power? Leaving that aside, surely this question, as well as the more general attempt to link 'mobilisation of bias' with power, is too vague in its existing form? We need to be rather more explicit.

When Schattschneider coined the expression 'mobilisation of bias', he did so specifically with reference to the nature of organisations. He was making the point that political objectives are achieved as much by the way in which interaction is structured as it is by the formulation and enactment of policy objectives. In other words, certain rules, processes, or structures will be established because they are intended to have certain routine effects. Parry and Morriss note that while 'Primacy should be given to the causal approach', the process of actor identification will often 'arrive back at a routine, and the analysis of routine raises different problems of analysis'.[63] But there are different types of routine, and some are more amenable to causal analysis than others. It makes a great difference to know whether the routine in question is based in custom, convention, or law. A mobilisation of bias which is founded in law can surely be regarded as an exercise of power by those who enacted the law – always provided the consequences are roughly what was intended. If the routine in question is customary then surely its effect cannot be regarded as an act of power – unless it was invoked, or performed with some other object in mind, in which case its description is no longer 'customary action'. It is wrong, therefore, to refer to the area of customary usage as if it could represent a mobilisation of bias since that is necessarily a conscious construct, and custom is certainly not that.

The question of 'mobilisation of bias' can be sharpened up by identifying the nature and basis of its legitimacy. Some biases are a lot more organised than others. The problem with this area of discussion, though, is that it is just too vague. There may well be, for example, 'an unwritten and unspoken code of conduct abroad in communities which would allow only the leaders to be vociferous and active in political affairs beyond community borders',[64] but whether this is a mobilisation of bias, and whether it can be regarded as an exercise of power can be answered only in a highly specific context. In other words we would have to be able to identify specific individuals who failed to speak out where we would have otherwise expected them to be vociferous, and we would then need to identify the mechanism by which the code of conduct had effect.

The analysis of action is complex for a variety of reasons. Because it may be routed through linkages spanning time and distance, it may not seem to provide the direct connection between actors apparently required by power theory.[65] But no one could seriously argue that power relationships are restricted within the confines of face to face interaction, nor deny that action may be structured in highly complex, and possibly devious, forms. Gaventa's reference to the American Association Ltd is a documented example, and Schattschneider's mobilisation of bias refers to a similar means of structuring action in complex forms.

Identification of relevant action also depends on establishing what it was that the others in the power interaction responded to. After all, if the outcome to be explained is a change in B's behaviour, then one essential piece of information in any explanation is the stimulus perceived by B. We have to understand the nature of B's perceptions, particularly since the image of collectivities may operate powerfully on the minds of others. Where we talk of power in simple dyadic terms there is no problem in identifying A's action as the relevant action. Life is not usually as simple as that, though, and the only way to identify the relevant action may be by asking B. Since actors are not always aware of the reasons for what they do – they may be unable to identify the action they have responded to, and have little clue as to the identity of the other actors – it is essential to locate inquiry within a well-grounded functional frame of reference. The possible elusiveness of this 'post-decision executive procedure', and of the figures behind it, demands that the observer's sensitivity to his subject should be as broadly, as well as sharply, defined as possible.

3 Intention

Most writers on power believe that it is necessary to incorporate data about actors' intentions in any analysis of power.[1] But serious objections are advanced which cause others to think differently. Some, for example, believe that making intention central to power overemphasises the importance of rational calculation; others, that reliable information to determine the subjective orientation of any actor is, in many cases, impossible to obtain, and easy to fake. Some believe that we should do without the term, while others urge that intention is simply not broad enough, and must be supplemented. It will be argued here that these objections are based on misinterpretations of what it means to say that something was intended. But if 'intention' is confirmed as at the core of any discussion of power, we are still left with very real problems of interpretation. Having disposed of the objections, then, an attempt will be made to show how these problems might be tackled.

(a) *Intention as rational consciousness.* This interpretation embraces the view that '*A* intends *x* when *A* has a clear-cut idea of what would count as "*x*"';[2] that '"intention" and related terms connote consciousness';[3] and that the debate 'encapsulates unsound assumptions about the extent to which political behaviour is calculated, deliberate and ratiocinative'.[4] When political behaviour is not ratiocinative, then it is just 'inappropriate to ask what the agent's intentions were'.[5] Arguing that intention must be interpreted in this way, Jack Nagel concludes that the concept is of no value to the study of power since it cannot apply to the power of anticipated reactions. In such a case, it will be recalled, *B* defers to what he believes are *A*'s wishes without any conscious attempt by *A* to secure that particular effect. Since this is generally agreed to be an example of *A*'s power, and since no intention (interpreted as conscious orientation) is apparent, then it follows that intention is not a universally necessary feature of power.

But is it reasonable to define intention in this way? Some writers think not. Robert Merton suggests, for example, that 'clearcut, explicit . . . awareness of purpose may be unusual, the aim of action more often than not being nebulous and hazy'.[6] Anthony Giddens is even more explicit:

> The most mundane forms of day-to-day conduct can quite properly be called intentional. It is important to stress this, since otherwise it might be tempting to suppose that routine or habitual conduct cannot be purposive (as Weber tended to do). However, neither intentions nor projects should be equated with *consciously held-in-mind* orientations towards a goal – as if an actor must be aware of an aim he is seeking to attain. Most of the stream of action which constitutes everyday conduct is pre-reflective in this sense.[7]

Over the whole range of learned behaviour, it is common to say that certain actions become second nature. We do not have to consciously formulate action as a response to a wide range of repetitive events. But an initiating act may not only establish an automatic response ability, it may also set up a standing condition (high status, wealth, aggressive appearance), or an organisation (New Haven Lawn Club, merchant bank, protection mobsters) that can be said to embody the initial intention. The existence of any of these is effectively a statement of intention to anyone who can read the signs, in the same way as the initiatory action or its subsequent copy. An intention may be given a variety of continuing forms. Wherever that form is invoked, engaged, or evokes an appropriate response, then we are justified in referring to the act as intended, whether or not there is any awareness on the part of the agent.

This interpretation is in line with the view generally taken by jurists. Some[8] try to avoid the intrusion of subjective judgement in interpreting the mental state of the accused by arguing that criminal guilt can be proved only by positively establishing that a form of rational consciousness could be held to apply. This would be in cases where the accused's act was voluntary; where he knew what he was doing; and where he had foresight of the prohibited consequences.

The majority view,[9] though, argues that, where the accused is proved to have committed the act, *mens rea* cannot be demonstrated where any one of various limiting conditions such as being an infant, insane or coerced, apply. In other words, where none of the limiting conditions holds, it is possible to argue that the state of the accused's mind is open to interpretation. The way in which this interpretation is proposed will not be debated here.[10] It is sufficient for the purposes of the present argument to note that jurists are prepared to argue that the negligent should be treated in law as if they had intended the actions in dispute.

(b) *Intention as essentially problematic.* An alternative objection is that 'intentions are hard to prove and hard to measure',[11] because 'the impossibility of direct access to what the other really meant, said, or intended'[12] means that 'the analyst must discover an actor's intentions from statements and actions that are frequently designed to mislead'.[13] John Champlin, however, argues as 'unnecessary the requirement that we know what is consciously present to [the agent's] mind at a given time'. It is enough that we know what 'descriptions of actions are available to him which are current in his social environment, providing he is not insane, idiotic or a child'.[14]

Stewart Clegg objects to such an approach on the grounds that it does not open up the actor's mind, but simply imposes 'common usage as a determinant of what things are . . . Common meaning may not be the key to interpretation so much as that which locks us within itself and outside of interpretation'.[15] Presumably Clegg means to say simply that we should not take 'common meaning' as a sure guide to interpretation. Merton suggests that:

> the observer's own experience and knowledge of the situation enables him to arrive at a solution. Ultimately the final test is this: does the juxtaposition of the overt action, our general knowledge of the actor(s) and the specific situation and the inferred or avowed purpose 'make sense', is there between these, as Weber puts it, a 'Verstandliche Sinnzusammenhang'.[16]

A moment's reflection will bring out whether we really want to discover the full essence of the power actor's meaning. Nagel supports his view that 'intention' should not be fundamental to our understanding of power by arguing that 'behavioral scientists should think twice before relying on a concept that arouses such contention in courts of law'.[17] The immediate response is that such difficulties have not resulted, and are not likely to result in the concept losing its importance for the courts. But that is in a sense a quite irrelevant answer. The social sciences have a different role. Whereas the law establishes, or represents, a fixed framework and is concerned only with the relationship of the individual to that framework, the framework created by the social scientist is uncertain, and the behaviour of the individual is of interest largely, or even entirely, to the extent that it can clarify that framework. Of course it is nice to 'get it right'. But everything that would have to be involved in getting it right would not necessarily be relevant to an observer's explanatory framework. Political science at any rate, is not likely to construct, or even to want to construct, a framework that sets out to exhaust comprehensively the meaning of a single action for a single individual.

The objection based on the inaccessibility of true meaning is singularly beside the point. Any social science must necessarily forego the full meaning of the actor. But it must on the other hand present an interpretation such that, *were the actor to accept that limiting framework*, he would say 'yes that is what I meant'. It goes without saying that the critical test of analysis lies in construction of the framework, but that framework is not necessarily best constructed by the actor. As MacIntyre puts it, 'The privileged position which the agent enjoys in respect of his actions is not such that the agent can explain his action better than anyone else'.[18] And the reason for this is given by Wittgenstein: 'an intention is embedded in its situation, in human customs and institutions. If the technique of the game of chess did not exist, I could not intend to play a game of chess'.[19]

(c) *Intention not an essential element of power*. A more sweeping objection is raised by Quentin Gibson who argues that if one wishes to describe power *tout court* then one must not include within that description any characteristics which do not apply to all the circumstances of our use of the word. One of the accepted uses of 'power' lies in its application to inanimate things. 'That a stormy sea has the power to wreck a ship or an engine the power to turn the wheels is surely something which no one should feel hesitant about maintaining'.[20] No one could now suggest, however, that there is an intentionality implied in such a description. If intentionality is not applicable in the case of inanimate power it does not, Gibson argues, apply in all cases. If it does not apply in all cases, the argument runs, it cannot be necessary to an understanding of power in the most general sense.

At this point it is worth taking up an interesting suggestion made by Gibson, and which he rather too lightly dismisses. In referring to inanimate power he notes that:

It may be said that this is anthropomorphism, and that in the literal sense only people have power. But this would be to confuse the origins of the concept with its nature. It may well be that in earlier and more animistic days, power, like causal efficacy, was attributable only to human or other spiritual agencies with wills. But generalization of the concept has taken place long since, certainly by the time of Hobbes and Locke. The move from human power to horse power, and from horse power to engine power, is a matter of history. And when a physicist defines the power of an engine in terms of the amount of work it can do in unit time, he need not concern himself with its intentions.[21]

There are two approaches that can be taken to Gibson's argument. Suppose, first, that the concept 'power' was, in earlier times, extended to inanimate matter on animist premises. Do we have to accept his curious implied conclusion that, because we are not animists, we therefore have grounds for changing the meaning of the concept? Do we have to accept that, although the animists were wrong about the nature of matter, they were nevertheless unknowingly right about their association of power with inanimate matter, and that this association should be seminal for any future understanding of political power? Surely we have no grounds for believing that the extension of a concept into new areas must necessarily weaken its meaning in its original sphere – even though Gresham's Law raises fears for its well-being. It can be argued, though, that Gibson has simply uncovered a homonym. There is after all, as if it needed pointing out, a significant qualitative difference between the animate and inanimate. Why should we expect the word power to have the same meaning in each case? The obliteration of intention from 'animate' power can be said to be just as false now as the animistic attribution of intention to inanimate objects was then.[22]

The linguistic side of Gibson's argument that intention is not a necessary element of power may, therefore, be rejected. Consider next the conclusions that Gibson draws from the argument. He cannot simply dismiss intentions – which he considers are irrelevant – and leave it at that. That would leave him with a view of power that is indistinguishable from cause, and he argues that 'there is something radically wrong with this identification'[23] since one can have power without exercising it. His preferred solution is to make power into a logical conditional dependent on some occasioning condition. 'To say that the policeman has the power to stop the traffic is to say that *if* some traffic came along and he held up his hand it would stop.'[24] Gibson argues, however, that it makes no difference to the attribution of power whether the occasioning condition is internal or external to the agent: 'the power to produce an effect remains the very same power even when it is manifested in different ways.'[25] To demonstrate his point he refers to the example of a careless smoker who constantly causes fires but never achieves anything he intends. In rejecting the view that such a person could not be called powerful, he appeals to 'normal usage'.

> The man is clearly able to cause fires, whether he actually intends to or not, and it is precisely in this that the regrettable power of such people lies. We might not say he was exercising his power because the word 'exercise' has a reference to intention built into it. But we would certainly say that the starting of the fires was a manifestation of his power.
>   It is true he would cause a fire if he tried. But his power does not consist in this; it could be manifested without his trying, by his flipping a butt negligently on to dry grass.[26]

Within the context of a discussion of the relevance of intention, what does it mean to say that the careless smoker demonstrates his power by accidentally causing a fire? If we can say that it was just not possible for the smoker to be aware of fire developing from this discarded butt then we must dismiss all question of intentionality, but we are left with the problem of describing the smoker's action. There must obviously be a 'certain kind of "break" in a series of action descriptions, after which "break" we cannot say that the agent is performing actions of those descriptions'.[27] Just as fire can be a consequence of the action of discarding a butt, so also may a whole line of future events. But, to indulge in a fanciful anachronism, just as the smoker was not signalling the approach of the Armada, nor, more mundanely, clearing the bush for planting, neither was he lighting a fire. Remember that it has been suggested that the possibility of fire resulting was just not foreseeable. If this is the case, then starting the fire was not his action. Where the occasioning condition is external to the supposed agent there is no relevant action. There could therefore be no exercise of power. Of course, we could not deny the statement 'he has the power to light fires' – where 'power' can be interpreted to mean 'ability'. But the demonstration of our power must meet a sharper test than accident, and cannot be dealt with as if it were simply a matter of strict liability. It is difficult to see how a power relationship could be said to exist between a careless smoker and an unforeseeable fire. It goes without saying that there is a causal relationship. But cause is not power, as Gibson accepts. All we can say of this example is that it demonstrates the power of fire.

Gibson's illustration of the unintended effect of the careless smoker bears as much weight in his argument as it does only because the example is so equivocal. It does not support his assertion because, depending on the foreseeability of the consequences, it was either not an act, or it was, in fact, intended. No *via media* between intention and cause has, therefore, been demonstrated.

(d) *Intention as too narrow a requirement*. D. M. White believes on the other hand that, rather than discarding intentionality, it should be added to:

> The issue, in its broadest terms, is what kind of attitude or state of mind an actor must have toward any given effects of his behaviour for it to be appropriate to say that he has exercised power with respect to them. I take it that there is no genuine issue about whether some state of mind (or analogue thereto) is required, for if there were, then a distinction between personal power and causation could hardly be sustained . . . The question must be *which effects besides intended ones are to be included*.[28]

In answering his own question, White makes two suggestions. The first modification occurs, he believes, where 'the effect results from an habitual act'.[29] This has already been briefly discussed in this section, where it was asserted that no distinction need be made between the orientation of an actor in developing a habit, and in the repetition of that habit. (I am referring here only to habitual action that is goal-oriented.) The point can be put more firmly, however, by examining the example on which White bases his argument.

Having distinguished between particular and general intentions, noting that an actor cannot be said to have the former in relation to an habitual act, White argues that 'he might have a general intention about the kind of result he wants to achieve when the relevant circumstances arise'.[30] On the other hand, where a minister makes a decision on a case without giving it any thought, he 'might act habitually . . . without having a general intention'.

> Habits may be formed in many ways: sometimes there is an initial decision based on some consideration of consequences, but at

other times the initial decision is taken without thought and the issue is never considered.[31]

The example that White gives of 'unthinking decision-making' is where a minister, confronting a standard problem for the first time, goes along with his adviser's recommendation then and on every future occasion. This is not, however, a very happy example. If we assume that the minister is reasonably competent and experienced, he would, in the moment of being confronted with problem and adviser (on whom he has probably already formed a judgement and, therefore, an intention as to their future relationship: e.g. 'I intend to trust him'), reach a decision based on some general intentions towards policy, administrative style, and political advantage. So to say that any skilled performer can perform within the area of his skilled competence without thought and intention is misleading. It is misleading precisely because the isolation of that moment of performance from what is necessary to produce it is quite unrealistic.

The second proposed modification that White makes to the intentional requirement is that it may simply be necessary for a favourable attitude to be present; 'it is enough that somewhere in his mind or in his feelings, no matter how deeply recessed, there was something which may be characterised as a favourable attitude'[32] which was present before the relevant outcome. White draws this conclusion on the basis of a lengthy analysis of five examples; 'only by attending to the details with great care is it possible to grasp the nuances of various states of mind and to comprehend their profound significance for the present subject.'[33]

In all the examples that White gives, analysis starts from an agent's action: the 'unthinking' decision of a minister; a prime minister's action in expelling an envoy; a successful candidate's first press conference; a prime minister's speech; and, of a different order, a mother's rearing of her child. He then outlines various possible scenarios to show how that action can be related to some outcome. His concern is to show that the relationship can, in some cases, best be described as 'hoped for' or 'wanted' rather than 'intended'. White does not suggest, however, that intentionality is unnecessary. He is simply pointing out that there are many occasions where the outcome is unpredictable, and where the prudent agent can do no more than hope. He does not dispose of intentional action as a necessary element of power. As he recognises, some action has to be performed with the intention of furthering those hopes.

What he is doing here is to acknowledge the problematic nature of the social and political reality within which power operates, and which is created by it. He has not qualified the meaning of power itself. No doubt there are relatively few instances which approximate the ideal statement of power exercise where an agent has an outcome firmly in mind, and acts successfully in its achievement. All this means is that there are probably few instances where an outcome can be attributed solely to the power of one agent. Engels wrote in his famous letter to Bloch of September 1890 that 'what each individual wills is obstructed by everyone else, and what emerges is something that no one willed'. This is too gloomy to swallow whole, but it is only partly wrong. The intractability of the socio-political medium is such that only fools and the omnipotent lack doubt. Apart from them, actors in a power process must hope. But 'hope' cannot be part of a definition of power that is additional to intention since hope is of the essence of intention. If intention were simply taken to mean 'rational consciousness' then it would probably be necessary to add White's rider. Since its meaning is broader, the rider is not required.

(e) *Intention and political science.* Intention, therefore, is a necessary element of power, and can be embodied in habitual action, standing conditions, or organisations. It can also be expressed in cases where the necessary causal element is present but the effect is simply 'hoped for', and even where the object of action is little more than a hazy idea covering a variety of alternative possibilities.

Robert Brown argues, though, that 'the place of intention-explanations in the social sciences is a modest one'[34] because 'individual actions – those of a given person – are usually interesting only as members of a class of actions'.[35] Such a view is, of course, damning for any attempt to place 'intention-explanation' at the heart of a concept which is so central to the social sciences. The argument has less force, perhaps, for political science. Individuals can occupy isolated political positions, wield considerable political power in their own right, and therefore play crucial roles.[36] But Brown is right in the sense that it may be very difficult to attribute to individual actors responsibility for the most intractable problems in politics.

Where, for example, Hunter discusses poverty, intentionality appears to fly out of the window, and the impression is given of a bizarre and incomprehensible conjunction of urbane, virtuous power, and wretched, dependent poverty:

The individual and his community, so far as the leaders are
concerned, is not a question of 'bad' men consciously being cruel
to helpless individuals. The leaders of Regional City are
individually very pleasant persons to meet, and many of them
appear to be good fathers, to attend church, and to have many of
the virtues ascribed to 'good' men. Few of them would publicly
say that the socially helpless should 'root hog or die'.[37]

Despite these virtues, the leaders of Regional City propose that the
problem is a federal one: 'they cannot face the demands . . . and
none feels individually responsible',[38] even though Hunter observes
that professional and other under-structure personnel speaking on
behalf of the underprivileged will be discouraged by 'warnings,
intimidations, threats, and in extreme cases, violence'.[39] Someone
intended, for whatever reason, that the 'socially helpless' should not
be helped. Can it also be said that they intended there should be
poverty? Surely if we were to make such a claim we would imply
that they actively sought to bring about such a state, and that they
can be held responsible for its existence – or, at least, for attempting
to bring it into existence, or to maintain it in existence when it
would otherwise have ceased. But, if 'the poor are always with us', it
would be as absurd to refer to intention with respect to poverty as it
is so plainly absurd to refer to it with regard to the location of the
South Pole.

  Where a state of affairs already exists we can say that someone has
intentions in relation to it under the following circumstances:

1. if they propose to change it;
2. if they support it against proposed changes;
3. if they create the conditions for its survival when it would
   otherwise fail.

This merely stakes out an area for discussion. We would need to
argue, for example, to what extent support for a condition can be
tacit and passive, and yet still manifest intention. Take, for example,
where a powerful party official intends to dispose of a party leader
whom he judges is a declining asset. If he acts on this and is
successful, we could say that a classic example of the actor –
intention – action – outcome sequence is demonstrated. If, however, another party official observes this process at work, and
understands perfectly what is going on, yet refuses to act one way or
the other, how should we judge his intentions? If it were perfectly

plain that inaction could only help the process of leader rejection and replacement, then anyone who consciously chooses this path, being aware of its consequences, must acquiesce in the outcome. Now there is a great gap between 'acquiescing' and 'intending'. Acquiescence is a passive condition, whereas intention necessarily denotes an active one. Yet part of the gap might be bridged if we recognise the nature of the relationship between the parties.

Consider the position of the average Atlanta citizen in relation to the following process referred to by Hunter:

> all car operators were deputized as special police and armed with revolvers. There was very little publicity on this action, but periodically the papers carried back page stories of Negroes who had been wounded or killed by the trolley operators. Violence is in this case a concomitant of policy, and policy within our definition is determined by the wills of men and is sanctioned within the social structure. Threats and statements designed to intimidate were followed in this case by the power-practice of violence.[40]

If in this case the average citizen was aware of the reason for deputising car operators as police, and arming them with revolvers, and agreed with that line of action, could we then say that he intended the subsequent outcome? Assume that the citizen had no connections with the political sphere. Surely it would be unreasonable to refer even to a 'supportive', as distinct from an 'initiatory', intention in a case where the subject could not affect the outcome except by action which is so extreme (e.g. murdering all relevant decision-makers) as to place it outside the limits of socially acceptable behaviour. Of course, the citizen's decision to be 'non-political' must be taken to mean that he had certain generalised intentions in relation to subsequent political action. If such a position were spelt out it could hardly do more than provide a very loose connection between the citizen and specific aspects of subsequent activity. For example, he could legitimately say that his inactivity had been predicated on certain assumptions, and that these did not cover the sort of action taken against negroes on public transport.

To judge if this were true, or probable, we need only consider what is 'sanctioned within the social structure'. No one in Atlanta at the time Hunter was writing could, it appears from Hunter's evidence, have doubted the general direction and intensity of repressive attitudes towards negroes. If there is a lack of involvement in a political system which is so distorted or biased that there can be no doubt as to the range of outcomes in relation to any problem, then surely the consequences cannot be described as unintended? Notice that this question has moved away from the third person singular. The uninvolved, powerless and acquiescent individual cannot be said to have intentions in regard to *any* specific action. It may well be that it is just misleading to test all questions of intentionality against specific outcomes, and to do so for specific actors. Such dogmatic empiricism would make it impossible to link the apparently inactive to the political system. At this point it may well be more sensible to abandon the concept 'intention' as being a necessary element of power. Or we might say that we are no longer talking about power, but some metaphysical property located in the social structure. Could that be what Hunter is referring to when he writes of:

> an unwritten and unspoken code of conduct abroad in communities which would allow only the leaders to be vociferous and active in political affairs beyond community borders.[41]

At first glance it would seem that this is beyond the scope of Hunter's definition of power which focuses on the 'acts of men . . . moving other men'. What is neither written nor spoken is likely to provide poor evidence about intentions. But such a code of conduct is interpreted by those subject to it as intending that they should limit their forms of political activity. And presumably the signs by which the code is interpreted do not come direct from the entrails of chickens, or the flight pattern of crows. They must come from the 'acts of men'. Such actions are plainly significant if they have the effect of de-politicising the majority of the community on extra-community affairs. Again, the problem is how to identify the relevant action, and how to link this in a satisfying manner to the intentions of identifiable actors.

At this point it is worth looking at the work of Robert Agger, Daniel Goldrich and Bert Swanson, who are the only writers in the community power literature to make specific reference to intention in their definition of power, and for whom the problem of such a linkage appears to be central.

Political power is a construct assigned to people on the basis of
their impacts on or contributions to outcomes and on the basis of
their purposes or intentions.[42]

They do not discuss their understanding of intention. But one of the
main objectives of their study of the power structure and political
regimes of four communities is to incorporate the perspectives of the
citizenry, and they attempt this through the concepts of preference,
ideology and interest. Now these are certainly not the same as
intention, but the question to be asked here is, How can we use them
to attribute power to individuals? How can preference, ideology, or
interest be used to indicate intention?

In opening their discussion of this problem, they note that 'the
decisional preferences of most citizens in the four communities
seemed to be more influenced by group and personal interests than
by ideology', and go on to ask 'What, then, was the importance of
'ideology?'[43] The answer, they believe, lies in the importance of
group activity; 'community politics was found to be largely group
politics. Relatively enduring groups of people were found to be
actively involved in the political decision-making of all four
communities'. Moreover 'a desire to maintain or impose an
ideology on the leaders of the community power structure . . . was
most intense in the key members of these political groups'. In their
view, ideology is important because it is a means by which
strategically located individuals screen interest-based proposals for
action. In this sense it is sufficiently important for Agger, Goldrich
and Swanson to claim that 'much of the variation in the politics of
the four communities is understandable only in the light of
variations within the ideological dimension'. In addition, they note,
this 'informal political organization of ideologically differentiated
groups' makes possible 'both extensive citizen participation in
politics and intensive conflict in decision-making', although they
are at pains to note that it is a 'necessary although insufficient
condition'.

If ideology is so salient for these 'inner cliques', then ideology can
be taken to serve as a convenient guide to what those actors'
intentions would have been in various community outcomes. We
would still need to provide the other crucial link between actor and
outcome through some evidence of action. But, once we have
established the nature and variety of ideologies in a community, we
have a basis for pursuing such action research that is grounded on an

understanding of the probable nature and intensity of intentions in that sector of the community.

Since 'the proportion of citizens in any of the four communities whose ideologies were of equal or greater importance than their interests was very small',[44] the foregoing strategy is of no value for establishing the power position of the majority in relation to any particular, or general outcome. For these the concept of 'interests' seems to be more relevant. But if individuals define their interests they provide a guide to their actions or intentions only in the immediate context in which the definition is provided. In certain circumstances two or more identified interests may be in conflict: in other words, one or more 'interests' may no longer be in their interests. For example, Crenson's study of two American steel towns cited in Chapters 2 and 4, suggests that the citizens of those communities could not pursue both of the fairly basic interests of full employment and a healthy atmosphere. The effect of imposing clean air legislation on the steel companies would, it was believed, be financially crippling and would lead to a cutback in production and employment.

We cannot, then, rank any person's interests in absolute hierarchic order. We cannot know, in advance of information about the specific situation in which the question 'what are his interests?' is put, what an individual's interests are, and, more important, how to establish priorities between them. Of course it is possible to make some highly generalised and universal statement such as Lockes' 'Civil interests I call life, liberty, health and indolency of body; and the possession of outward things such as money, lands, houses, furniture and the like'.[45] But, in any given instance, it could be shown, that an individual's interests might lie in denying any or all of these. No useful statement of interests can, therefore, ignore the situation in which those interests are defined. Nor can it, for our purposes, ignore any reference to the outcomes selected as focal points for a study of power. We are obliged, therefore, not to establish an individual's interests *tout court*, but to settle what his interests are in relation to any given outcome.

There is a further problem posed by nominating 'interest' as a possible means of providing an intentional link between actor and outcome. In the case of ideology there is no question but that whatever *A* says is his ideology (provided he is not lying) is truly *A*'s ideology. We do not, of course, imply any judgement about the origin of these beliefs, nor about their appropriateness to *A*'s objective situation. In the case of an individual's interests, though, it may not be possible to determine these solely by reference to what he says they are. It is commonplace to observe that what *A* wants may not be in his interests. But, if we are arguing that, as with ideology, we should be able to provide a bridge between interest and intention, how, we might ask, is this possible if we argue that *A*'s interests are obscured from him, yet are discoverable by reference to objective criteria? An actor cannot be motivated by an interest of which he is not aware.

The question hinges on the nature of an actor's unawareness. If this is absolute then there can be no question of meaningful orientation and, therefore, no question of that actor being said to exercise power. But an actor is able to protect or further his interests without being aware at any given point precisely what those interests are. He may employ an agent, elect a representative, or join a group for the purpose. In other words, the actor may do something with the further intention that that action shall, in some way as yet indeterminable, be in his interests. Hart describes this as an example of an 'oblique intention', where 'the agent had control over the alternative courses of action and knowingly chose one'.[46]

This, of course, raises the question of what we might mean by 'control over'. For example, a voter presented with a choice between a moderate conservative and a right-wing socialist candidate might argue that his control had been pre-empted. But leaving that question aside as one to be resolved case by case, and ignoring the further question of determining how actions purportedly in the principal's interests can be shown to be in his interests, the general point made here is straightforward. Individuals try to protect their interests in various ways. Some of these will be more indirect than others. It is the observer's job to identify these. The fact that any given individual appears not to be meaningfully oriented towards actions performed in his interests does not mean that there is no intentional link.

It is worth re-stating the problem at this point. There is no difficulty in linking an action with outcome in a way that satisfies Agger, Goldrich and Swanson's notion of power where we have direct evidence of intention through statements or whatever; or where we have indirect evidence through ideological commitment or through interests shared by members of a group on whose behalf someone has acted. This is not to say, of course, that ideology and interest point to clearly distinct phenomena and that, where we identify an ideology, we can ignore any contrary pull from interests. Agger, Goldrich and Swanson cite the hypothetical case of a proposal by city government to establish municipal parking-lots in the downtown business district. The way in which those business-men affected would react would vary. Some would be ideologically opposed to the concept of active government, particularly in the economic sphere, yet would support the scheme because of the probable increase in business that it would bring. For some, ideological commitment would over-ride shrewdly perceived busi-ness interest, while others could perhaps be described as non-ideological pragmatists, ready to take what opportunity offers, or as ideologically naive and unable to interpret the significance of what is happening.

Such an example demonstrates the problems of interpreting motivation and purpose, of the possible confusion of ideology and interest, as well as the importance of fully understanding the context. Yet so long as there is an ideological framework, or a group structure within which interests can be understood, we have a means of linking individuals to action. Where there is neither ideology nor group structure then the problem of interpretation is extremely difficult. Solo parents, asthmatics, or 'members' of an economic class, can be said to share interests, yet may be linked neither organisationally nor ideologically. In what sense would it be possible to identify a relevant outcome – for example, that their interests in a particular respect had been over-ridden or overlooked – and then argue that their 'common' interests necess-arily place them in some power relationship to the outcome? How could we argue that they are, in that case, powerless simply on the grounds that they would surely have intended otherwise had they been aware of the process leading to the outcome?

We can, of course, argue that anyone who fails to pursue their own interests must, by definition, be powerless. But this is unsatisfactory. The identification of interests by solely objective criteria cannot tell us anything about the orientation of the actors concerned. We would need a very different approach to power from that proposed by Agger, Goldrich and Swanson before we could throw this subjective dimension out of the window. Perhaps the answer is simply to resort to one of Weber's two forms of *Verstehen*. The first form, *aktuelles Verstehen*, suggests that it is possible to derive 'the meaning of an act or symbolic expression from immediate observation without reference to any broader context.' The other form, *erklärendes Verstehen*, points to the necessity of placing any particular act, including socially oriented inaction, 'in a broader context of meaning involving facts which cannot be derived from immediate observation of a particular act or expression'.[47] This second form, which Parsons translates as 'explanatory understanding', is directly appropriate to the problem of interpreting the subjective meaning for any given actor, or aggregate of actors, of interests arbitrarily attributed to them. If we want to reconstruct an actor's probable subjective orientation towards some actual outcome, we have to rely on contextual data.

What emerges from juxtaposing intention with interest and ideology is that, in addition to the more obvious sources of information concerning an actor's intention, we may add ideological position, group interest and, possibly, a broader interpretation of interest in which intention has to be inferred from a much looser collection of social facts. It is, no doubt, partly as a correction to this 'looseness of facts' that Agger, Goldrich and Swanson propose a means of classifying the relationship between the citizen and his societal environment. Four categories are put forward that 'refer to the institutionalized ways of organizing the production, distribution, and consumption of (1) wealth; (2) civic amenities; (3) social status, respect, affection, or prestige; and (4) governmental rights and obligations of citizenship'.[48] Where the perspectives of the actors are regarded as crucial to an enquiry then it is sensible to have a framework that attempts to take those perspectives into account in a systematic way. Dahl and Polsby proposed that it was sufficient to focus on selected areas of community life, defined in terms of overt and important activity.[49] Hunter resigned the problem in favour of a preoccupation with the affairs of those with a reputation for power. By contrast, the approach discussed here is at once broader as well as being more discriminating.

The difficulty of identifying intentions means that conjecture and assertion in any specific case must be placed within an explicitly formulated framework. Although the concept appears to be essentially individualistic, it is grossly misleading to formulate a picture of actors-with-intentions operating in processes that are otherwise devoid of intentionality. To do so is to trap political discourse in the 'push-and-shove, bump-and-grind mechanistic understanding of power and causation'[50] in which actors propel actions towards objectives, with intentions occupying roughly the same place in the sequence as a cue in the game of billiards.

Intentions may be manifest in a variety of forms. Explanation, therefore:

> requires a grasp of the complex of meaning in which an actual course of understandable action thus interpreted belongs. In all such cases, even when the processes are largely affectual, the subjective meaning of action, including that also of the relevant meaning complexes, will be called 'intended' meaning.[51]

The discussion of intention need not focus on the individual, even though it is a description of an individual state. Intention can be attributed to a group – without, it should be added, any implications of 'group mind' creeping in. Brown objects to such an attribution because of 'the difficulty of showing that *all* members of a group consciously had the aim in question or had some other aim which led them to the action, or had any aim at all'.[52] The view that an intention must be consciously formulated has been rejected here, so part of the force of Brown's argument disappears. For the rest, it is obvious that the problem of conclusively demonstrating the mental state of every actor in a group will escalate with the numbers involved. In many cases – particularly in historical research – the question just cannot be tested.[53] But is this what a comment about group intention really sets out to do? Surely it is nothing more than an 'as-if' statement. For example, in the absence of overt signs of dissension we can treat the Cabinet as if all the members intended to cut defence spending. On occasions when dissent is stifled our judgement will be wrong. But omniscience is no test of a social scientist's fitness.

4 Outcome

The problem of treating intention in the way that Allison, Nagel, White and Brown want is that it tends to isolate actor from context. Intentions are often difficult to identify, and the quick way to overlook them is to focus only on the conscious formulations of individual actors. Any approach to power that regards intentions as essential must show the extent to which they are achieved. Even if a power approach were not to regard intentionality as a necessary element, though, there can be no question but that some form of outcome must be involved. The term 'power' cannot be used without reference to an effect. This applies as much in the case of the possession of power as it does in the more obvious case of its exercise. If we want to identify the power possessed by an actor, we have to specify the type of effects by reference to which that potential is to be identified as power. As van Doorn puts it, 'it is impossible to possess or exercise power unless there is an object on which it bears'.[1]

Identification of outcome is, therefore, the necessary starting point in any demonstration of power. This is a requirement that has been overlooked in the major studies of community power. Researchers have either been preoccupied with establishing the nature of a power structure, as in Floyd Hunter's *Community Power Structure*, or with describing a power process, as in Robert Dahl's *Who Governs?* But such preoccupations do not necessarily lead into an analysis of actor motivation. Where Hunter and Dahl refer to the objectives of political action, their treatment is weak. Hunter, for example, refers to the setting up of an International Trade Council in Atlanta, but does not consider its effect, and does not explore the intentions of its founders.[2] Similarly the Plan of Development, a scheme for annexing areas of the urban spread of Atlanta which had grown up beyond the city boundaries, remains unexamined both in terms of its meaning to participants, and in terms of its consequences.[3] In looking at urban redevelopment in New Haven, Dahl focused on the activities of Mayor Richard Lee, whose commitment to redevelopment was fuelled by experience during his unsuccessful 1951 mayoral campaign. Dahl quotes Lee as follows:

> I went into the homes on Oak Street and they set up neighbor-
> hood meetings for me. I went into block meetings . . . three and
> four in one night. And I came out from one of those homes on Oak
> Street, and I sat on the curb and I was just as sick as a puppy.
> Why, the smell of this building; it had no electricity, it had no gas,
> it had kerosene lamps, light had never seen those corridors in
> generations. The smells . . . It was just awful and I got sick. And
> there, there I really began.[4]

Dahl does not suggest that this was the only reason for Lee's initiatives in 'an urban redevelopment program unmatched in the country' for a city of its size.[5] But Lee's reminiscence makes plain that the provision of satisfactory alternative accommodation must have been one of the outcomes that he sought to achieve by his action. Because Dahl does not say what happened to the inhabitants of Oak Street, though, he tells only part of the story, and his comments on power are partial. Lee may have been able to swing the vote in the council chamber and elsewhere, but did he have the power to achieve what he set out to do?

Peter Bachrach and Morton S. Baratz reacted against the approaches of Hunter and Dahl on the grounds that they over-looked a major problem in the study of power. They have formulated an alternative approach which 'tends to reverse the basic question. Rather than asking, Who rules? it asks, What persons or groups in the community are especially disfavored under the existing distribution of benefits and privileges?'[6] Such a focus would seem to be precisely what is required by an outcomes approach. But their methodology is remarkably like Dahl's which focuses on the formal decision-making arena as the criterion for the identification of power.[7] In pursuing the problem of the 'dis-favored', they simply propose that the arena of decision-making be widened to include the issue formation and policy implementation processes.[8]

Steven Lukes rejects the behavioural emphasis of Bachrach and Baratz's decision-making approach,[9] but shares with them the belief that the test of power lies in its effect. He proposes, therefore, that the harming of an individual's interests should be the critical focusing device.[10] The view taken here is that casting the power actor in the baleful role of aggressive misanthrope is altogether too restrictive. He refers to White in support of his interpretation of power as a form of significant affecting.[11] White does not limit the question of significance in the way that Lukes does, but proposes that the affecting must 'be significant either for whoever achieves it, or for whoever is affected'.[12] Furthermore, he nowhere suggests that the form of affecting be adverse. He argues that the 'formulation of a conceptual problem should leave open everything that is arguable, and should foreclose everything that is not'.[13] One aspect of power which is certainly arguable is whether it applies only to situations of coercion and conflict where interests are harmed, or whether it can also be used to describe the force generated by co-operative effort in relation to a shared problem.[14]

So the sole relevant type of outcome to be identified is not simply 'harmed interests', although in any given study where that is the extent of the observer's interest in power it may well be so. If we are considering the methodological requirements of a study of power at their broadest – leaving open everything that is arguable – then there is no justification for restricting the concept 'outcome' in any way other than by White's notion of 'significant affecting'. White's approach must not be taken to mean, though, that this is a requirement limiting the study of power to certain facts, but rather an injunction that the study of facts has to be presented in a certain way if it is to be considered a study of power. Lukes' argument can be criticised, not because it proposes 'interests' as a suitable topic for power analysis, but because it elevates the concept to sole discriminatory status. 'Interests', however, are simply a special case of a broader category, which includes 'decisions', 'processes' and 'events' as well. All of these are subsumed under 'outcome'.

The question of whether power analysis should move beyond preoccupation with decision-making to include reference to what Bachrach and Baratz call the 'Who Benefits?' alternative to the 'Who Governs?' approach[15] was considered by Nelson Polsby. His conclusions are as follows:

(1) value distributions occur without explicit decisions taking place, hence may tell us nothing about decision-making; (2) values within the community may be distributed in important ways as a by-product of decisions and nondecisions made outside the community; (3) there are many irrationalities in decision-making, which may lead to the distribution of values in

unpredictable, unintended ways; (4) the powerful may intentionally distribute values to the nonpowerful.[16]

These comments are essentially negative because Polsby assumes that the proper objective of power analysis is to understand the nature and consequences of the decision-making process, whereas the assumption here is that it should be to understand the intentional causes of any given outcome. Allen Schick points out that the pluralists assume that 'if the process is working properly, the outcome will be favourable. Hence there is no need for an explicit examination of outcomes'.[17] Michael Parenti agrees with Schick's criticism of the pluralist position:

> To study only the antecedent strategems of a given decision is to impose a rather imperfect understanding of 'process', one which does not recognize that outputs are as essential to an understanding of political process as inputs.[18]

In this broader perspective it is quite inadequate for Polsby to persist with an approach that restricts the scope of power analysis; inflates the significance of a particular type of actor; tends to over-emphasise the extent to which public affairs can be controlled; distorts the meaningful orientation of the actors involved who, unless they are either idiotic or naive, will not believe that legislation ends the story; and almost completely obliterates the role of the public bureaucracy. It is true that Polsby admits that 'not all conceivable questions or important questions about community politics can be answered by correct answers to the question "Who Governs?"'[19] In view of the significance of the questions it does not answer we may legitimately wonder at the value of the special position he is defending. His argument is mounted as an attack on claims made by Bachrach and Baratz, and Matthew Crenson, on behalf of the 'mobilisation of bias'. He argues that 'actual empirical inquiry must take place in which findings are made and the methods for making them explained and defended'.[20] This is a worthwhile injunction, but it does not demand an exclusive preoccupation with constitutionally established decision-making processes, particularly if their consequences are ignored.

The separate criticisms that Schick and Parenti make of the pluralist position do not discriminate in their use of the terms 'output' and 'outcome'. Frank Levy, Arnold Meltzner and Aaron

Wildavsky, however, have distinguished among decisions, outputs and outcomes in the following way. Decisions are seen as 'choices among alternative courses of action'; outputs are 'goods and services supplied by a public agency and received by (or directed at) the public'; and outcomes are seen as 'consequences of outputs'.[21] Consider now how we might characterise the meaningful orientation of an actor at these various stages. At the level of decision, the actor's intention will be 'this bill should be enacted'. At the level of output the actor's intention will be 'the terms of this bill shall be put into effect'. And at the level of outcome the actor's intention must be 'effecting this bill shall do the job it was intended to do'.[22]

This distinction is simple and compelling. Decisions are the necessary prerequisites of outputs, but explain only a subset of outcomes. Every decision has an output and outcome, and every output has an outcome. But, because of the significance of unintended effects, not all outcomes can be regarded as the intended product of outputs. This expresses in a rather tedious manner some of the general principles that are obscured by Polsby's practised defence of a decision-making approach in response to the woolly thinking that damages the justifiable concern of the nondecision-making lobby. If we concentrate power analysis on decisions and outputs we exaggerate the extent to which affairs can be controlled, and we, therefore, increase the expectations of political action. Outcome analysis is a more balanced approach to the study of power, as well as a more responsible one.

Whether a phenomenon is to be viewed as a decision, or an output, or an outcome, depends on the interests of the observer, and on the orientation of the actor. A phenomenon cannot be a decision if it is not intended, but can be regarded as the output of a decision-making process if we are concerned, for example, with evaluating the productivity of such a process. And equally the same decision can be seen as an outcome if we believe that it represents the end of a process. It may be useful, and perfectly legitimate, for some purposes to treat a decision as an outcome. But in the context of a study of power it tends to restrict relevance to statements about power relations within the decision-making body itself, and so is therefore ill-suited to a study of community power. Questions about 'outcome' may be trivial because researchers have trivial preoccupations. Where their concerns are complex, analysis must reflect that complexity or distort what it sets out to explain.

The obvious difficulty lies in deciding at what point the results of a process can be called an outcome. There is, after all, a note of finality about the term. Outcomes come at the end, but it is not always clear where that is. If we choose a midway point we ignore the integrity of an encompassing process that has meaning to its participants. If 'outcome' is defined without reference to the perspectives of the participants, any associated research will necessarily distort and misunderstand the nature of their action.

Where an outcome is the product of a short-term process in which objectives have been clearly stated, the problems of demonstrating a relationship between actor and outcome are small. In that case power is transparent. Where we have a long-term, complex process in which the relationship between variables and events is unclear, in which it is not possible to say with any degree of certainty to what extent an outcome was, or was not, dependent on some power act: in such a case how can we possibly make any claims about the operation of power? The short answer is that we do so on the basis of expectations derived from our own particular view of the world, and of ideas we have about a normal, or desirable, path of events. We believe that, if things had been left to themselves (whatever that might mean in practice) a different state of affairs would have come about. We argue, that is, on the basis of counterfactual statement.

Lukes was the first contributor to the community power debate to draw explicit attention to the importance of counterfactuals. He stated that 'any attribution of the exercise of power . . . always implies a relevant counterfactual'.[23] By this he meant that any attribution of power necessarily refers to an outcome that would not otherwise have occurred. Counterfactual statement simply draws attention to that possibility. It is an application of the principle of falsifiability.[24] No amount of evidence can conclusively prove that an assertion about power is true: it simply holds until disproved. If we can show that, on existing evidence, an assertion cannot be disproved, or, to put it in a way that is less open to misinterpretation, that the balance of probability in its favour cannot be shifted, then it can stand until further testing. The problem of evidence is, of course, greatest where the evidence for the outcome is weakest. Where, for example, we say that the outcome is inaction – not of a straightforward hiatus in an observed sequence, but the non-occurrence of a unique possibility – and where this is to be explained by the anticipated reactions of the power subject, so that the power actor engages in no overt action – this is the sort of example where a demonstration of the counterfactual is most urgent.

What is involved in making counterfactual statements? Jon Elster suggests that 'they doubly require a *theory*: both as a filter for assessing the legitimacy of the antecedent and as a deductive machinery for getting from the antecedent to the consequent'.[25] Consider, for example, the problem with the antecedent condition in the formulation 'if US Steel had not exerted power, Gary would have adopted clean air measures sooner'. This requires some justification of the notion that in the nearest possible world to Matthew Crenson's Gary there could either have been a Gary where US Steel did not have the same presumed impact, or where there was no US Steel at all.[26] If the company were removed entirely, the dirty air – and Crenson's study – would also have to go. But the alternative antecedent may simply require the removal of a single company representative, and is therefore quite legitimate.

Take instead the case of downtown development in Dahl's New Haven. We could reasonably say that 'if Mayor Lee had not pushed the redevelopment issue, it would not have been adopted'. Lee's commitment, as Dahl's narrative shows, was clear, and he was dramatically successful at the polls because of it.[27] Whether we can accept the antecedent condition, then, depends on whether we can visualise New Haven politics in the 1950s without Lee, or perhaps simply without a Lee who was committed to redevelopment. This sort of mental experiment presents no problems. We certainly do not have to follow through all the myriad implications that the removal of Lee, or the restructuring of his political interests, would in practice have involved. This would lead to what Barry calls 'irrelevant concretization'.[28] Neither alternative poses any problems for the fabric of New Haven politics that would require any changes in the way that redevelopment would normally come about. Establishing the antecedent is a problem only when the assumptions that have to be made to accept it would destroy the validity of the consequences, as in the case of visualising the course of the Second World War if Hitler had not existed. But this is a straightforward problem that does not involve anything said elsewhere in this discussion of power.

Of more interest is the second problem identified by Elster. Having established the antecedent, how do we get from there to the postulated consequent? Returning to the example of Mayor Lee, evidence presented by Dahl amply bears out the view that redevelopment was 'in the air', and that various converging threads gave some impression of inevitability to the process.[29] This would suggest that it would not be legitimate to accept the consequent – that redevelopment would not have occurred without Lee's initiative. Lee may have imparted some special flavour to the scheme that was adopted, but it seems that redevelopment was inevitable.

What would have to be involved in a theory that redevelopment could have occurred without Lee? The comments that have been made above about the various core elements being crucial to any analysis of power apply just as much to the test of the counterfactual. For example, it is not enough to assert that others would have acted on redevelopment if Lee had not, simply because 'redevelopment was in the air'. These are rather vague grounds on which to dismiss Lee from centre stage. We must ask instead whether we can point to any actors who intended, or embodied the intention, to redevelop. And we would have to be able to show how such action could have come about. All of this means that we have to have a firm idea of the framework within which action is typically cast.

Quite possibly the type of information pointed to in the previous paragraph will not be available. Crenson tries to get from the antecedent to the consequent by adopting a comparative technique. His argument is, in effect, that action could have been expected in the case of community *A* because of its similarity to another community, *B*, which did act. When comparison is being made at the level of communities, though, we must be very sensitive to the complexities involved. Young suggests that 'comparison fails when units are large'.[30] Size certainly adds to the difficulties, as a look at Matthew Crenson's study will show.

Crenson sought to answer the question why some American cities failed to act against air pollution when their objective circumstances suggested that they ought to have acted. This failure to act when it appeared so plainly to be in their best interests to improve the quality of the air being breathed is regarded by Lukes as constituting a relevant counterfactual. 'There is good reason to expect that, other things being equal, people would rather not be poisoned.'[31] Crenson's interest in these two particular towns was aroused because East Chicago acted early and swiftly – a dirty air bill was passed into law by the City Council in 1949 – whereas Gary acted tardily, producing no comparable measure until December 1962.[32]

Consider the nature of the problem. After comparing the state of pollution in the two towns, Crenson proposed that the antipollution measures adopted in East Chicago in 1949 were blocked in Gary until 1962. The evidence is comparative. All people should act against pollution, but the timing of such action is set in this case by East Chicago. It is crucial, then, that Crenson should be systematically explicit about what is being compared. We can, after all, properly regard Gary's absence of action as a failure to act only if it can be demonstrated that both towns could have been expected to move at the same speed. If they differ in marked respects we should not, perhaps, expect the same response. In which case the absence of action in any year between 1949 and 1962 could not be taken as a failure to act, and the counterfactual statement would collapse.

What Crenson is comparing is two different forms of community action, and it is central to his comparative purpose to establish the nature of these actors – i.e. communities. It is important to establish in what ways they are similar. This he does in terms of age, education, income and race. 'The survey findings from St Louis (showed) that citizens' concern about dirty air is related' to these variables.[33] But, although he finds that, in these terms, the two towns were closely comparable, in other respects the communities appear to differ markedly. East Chicago was relatively small (60,000 population) and crowded. Gary had three times the population (180,000) dispersed over a proportionately larger area, with some physical separation between factory and home. There are three factors here, then, which might have been significant, but which Crenson did not pursue – relative size of community, degree of crowding, and awareness of industry. The first two of these, at least, could be expected to shape power structure, but may operate independently of it. Crenson notes, though, that 'a more substantial difference existed in racial composition: in 1960 about 39 per cent of Gary's residents were non-white, while the figure for East Chicago was only 24 per cent'.[34] There would have been rather more point to such information if we had been given comparative data for the 1940s when East Chicago acted and Gary did not. If Gary's black population was significantly larger at that stage than East Chicago's, then we may assume that there was a greater propensity to non-participation built into the Gary political system. This is not advanced as a single explanation – if there is, in fact, anything to explain. But if such a factor did apply, then it would not be significant because of the power of some local agent, but because a very high proportion of blacks in America at the time had a very low sense of political efficacy. The answer would be found in the national system, and not locally. Beyond this, Crenson notes:

> an additional dissimilarity between the two towns which over-shadows all the others. While East Chicago's population grew by only 6 per cent between 1950 and 1960, Gary's increased by one-third. A similar difference is recorded for the decade 1940 to 1950, when Gary's population grew by almost 20 per cent while East Chicago suffered a slight decline. East Chicagoans have a simple explanation for the fact that their city has virtually stopped growing: there is simply no more space available in the town.[35]

This points towards yet another way in which the two towns differed and because of which Crenson may not have been justified in identifying inaction in Gary during the 1940s and 1950s as indicative of the operation of some local power source and, therefore, as constituting an outcome. East Chicago's more compact and established population seems better suited to being described as a settled community. Its internal dynamics would have been very different from those of the larger, more diffuse, and changing mixture of Gary. We would have every reason to believe that the responses of the two towns to an apparently identical problem would be different. In fact it would be very surprising if they were the same. Differential response might then be attributable more to generalised features of social interaction.

The evidence that Crenson puts forward to establish dirty air in Gary as a potentially relevant counterfactual is simply East Chicago's action in 1949. East Chicago is taken as the norm. But the brief review of Crenson's data on the two towns suggests the inappropriateness of that standard. This means that Crenson's subsequent exploration of the mechanism of nondecision-making in Gary is singularly inappropriate. He has not shown that there is any case to answer. Of course individuals had pollution problems of the same order. But the community responses to those problems were likely to differ. Crenson argues that:

> In spite of the political passivity, U.S. Steel seems to have had the ability to enforce inaction on the dirty air issue. Apprehension about the company's reaction to pollution control proposals may even have been responsible for Gary's late start in the pollution field.[36]

If the community could not have been expected to generate a response, however, the role assigned to US Steel becomes bizarre. Crenson does refer to other possible explanations – differences in local party organisations; in opportunities to register complaints; in political agendas; in skill of political actors; and in the role of state and federal agencies.[37] His subsequent statistical analysis of the responses to interviews with ten political leaders in each of fifty-one cities was designed to test the possible significance of this limited range of alternative explanations. In an otherwise enthusiastic review, Newton points out, however, that the statistical basis for Crenson's conclusion that inaction over pollution can be attributed primarily to the influence of local industry is surprisingly weak. And Polsby concludes that he does 'not think we can place very much confidence in Crenson's findings'.[38]

Lukes' claim that Crenson has identified a relevant counter-factual is unfounded. In fact, Crenson's account of the counter-factual is so cursory as to leave unclear what he was trying to explain. He starts from a notion of *individual* interests, and then tries to pursue this notion by examining why *communities* fail to act on the dirty air issue. In comparing Gary and East Chicago the question becomes confused and confusing because the comparative relationship is not explored and there is no indication of the significance of taking East Chicago as providing the behavioural norm.

Another example of a study where the demonstration of a counterfactual is important is John Gaventa's analysis of power in an Appalachian Valley.[39] This is more complex than Crenson's study since the relevant action took place over a much longer period of time, and the outcome is a much more generalised condition. Gaventa sets out to show that the poverty and insecurity experienced by the people of the Clear Fork Valley since the late nineteenth century can be attributed to the policy of mining companies, chief among which is the London-based American Association Ltd. The difficulty with his study is that it is never clear what his target population is. Certainly his sympathies are with the miners of Clear Fork Valley, but the overlap between them and the 'oppressed community'[40] of Clear Fork Valley is not made clear. It is not mere pedantry to require an identification of the central 'character'. Gaventa puts together such a description, though, by making reference to a variety of surrogates: 'the Appalachian case', Middlesboro, the Cumberland Gap area, Yellow Creek Valley, Claiborne County, District 19 of the United Mineworkers of America, and so on.[41]

This is not to contest Gaventa's general thesis that the American Association Ltd has acted oppressively, creating poverty, insecurity and a sense of powerlessness among some, possibly the majority, of the locals. The thesis is that, in the absence of that company, those same people would have been able to act in their own interests. Now although there seems a healthy ring of common sense about such a proposition, we need the reassurance that comparative evaluation can give. We need to be shown that other communities do, in fact, pursue interests that have been abandoned in the case of Clear Fork Valley. And we need, in particular, to be shown that these communities are comparable in ways that seem important to the question at hand. The reason for this is straightforward. The internal dynamics of some communities may well make the pursuit of self interest highly problematical, regardless of the external circumstances. We just have to be able to recognise, and understand the significance of, differences. It is, after all, important to know which oyster has the pearl, and which apple the worm. But we cannot put the question until we have decided what it is we are looking for, pearl or worm.

In Gaventa's case, although it is clear that his sympathies lie with the poor and dispossessed of Clear Fork Valley, it is not clear what collective noun describes them, nor what the characteristics of that collectivity might be. Gaventa has analysed the mine owners' impact on an undisclosed number of individuals representing an undisclosed proportion of the undisclosed total population of an undocumented community. What is needed is a straightforward classification of the object under study. Precisely who, and what, makes up the Clear Fork Valley community? Where such data is not provided, there is no proper basis for comparison, no secure grounds on which to establish the accuracy of a counterfactual, and no means of establishing that the outcome was dependent on a power act. Again, it is not suggested that any evidence produced in this way is likely to overthrow Gaventa's conclusions. What is suggested, however, is that without this information, the nature of the problem, and possibly the requirements for practicable change, cannot be properly understood.

After all, the people that Crenson and Gaventa are referring to are not isolated individuals. Most will be part of various solidary social relationships, and their behaviour will be as much oriented towards, and in part determined by, these as by the apparently compelling demands of external events. Their actions just cannot be explained solely by reference to one or two selected features of their environment, no matter how overwhelmingly important these features may seem to well intentioned outside observers.

Crenson and Gaventa have both identified politically significant outcomes – dirty air and poverty. In neither case has the counter-factual claim been sufficiently well established. Crenson's study, for example, offers no evidence that Gary was sufficiently like East Chicago for the latter to be used as a predictive model. And in Gaventa's study, the principal actor, Clear Fork Valley, pursues a shadowy existence that baulks any attempt at comparative evaluation and validation. In both cases there is as much cause for critical comment of the way in which the study is structured as there is in the case of the much contested earlier studies of Hunter and Dahl. Crenson and Gaventa do represent an advance, however, in that they move beyond the preoccupation with decision-making that has marked the work of elitist as well as pluralist researchers.

One thing that is clear from a discussion of counterfactuals is that it draws attention to the difficulty of proof in the social sciences, and to the consequent need to take the problem of falsifiability seriously. Any statement about power necessarily involves a counterfactual. But not every type of counterfactual is adequate for a thorough-going analysis of power. We can distinguish, for example, between 'in-process' counterfactuals such as conflict, sanction or decision, and 'end-process' counterfactuals, such as interests and outcome. In the former case the problem of verification is small, but the information thus provided is only part of what we need to know to understand power in that case – unless we choose to identify conflict, sanction or decision as the outcome to be studied. The consequence of doing that, though, may be to underestimate the complexity of power phenomena.

Although complexity is a very real difficulty, the comparison that counterfactual statement necessarily entails presents problems at a more fundamental level. Crenson tries to show that Gary would have adopted a clean air measure sooner in the absence of US Steel by offering East Chicago as a similar community which was able to act against dirty air. The critical difference is that pressure was exerted by US Steel in one case, but not in the other. So the counterfactual statement becomes, 'if US Steel had not exerted power, Gary (if it had been the same in all relevant respects as East Chicago) would have adopted a clean air bill sooner'.

The immediate problem, of course, is to determine what we mean by 'in all relevant respects'. If we accept Barry's injunction against 'irrelevant concretization', we must still have some criteria for judging whether a comparison is valid or not. And if we decide in what respects two communities should be comparable, we have to make clear whether our argument is being developed along the lines of structural determinism, or of structural correlationism. In the first case we are saying that explanation is possible by the identification of causal laws embedded in, or forming, the encompassing structure. This is rather more than Crenson or Gaventa would claim, who are no structural determinists. The point is that anyone who adopts such an approach must necessarily devalue, or completely ignore, the perspectives of the participants since they are no more than structural co-ordinates. But if our approach simply proposes a correlation between aspects of structure and behaviour, then structure is no longer a causal explanation of behaviour, but simply a means by which behaviour might more usefully be interpreted. In taking this alternative approach we are denying objective status to the structural framework within which our outcome has been located, and accepting the critical role of the participants themselves. If we do not accommodate their perceptions, we are – like it or not – infiltrating an element of structural determinism that is suspiciously like a covert ideological stance.

What can we conclude from all this? Most obviously, the study of power requires a focusing device, but one which does not restrict the scope of inquiry, as is the case with 'decision'. 'Outcome' serves this purpose and, therefore, locates power analysis in a more realistic setting that avoids overemphasising the extent of political control, as is the case with the decision-making approach. Beyond this, though, the fact that 'outcome' does not have the pseudo-objective status that can be accorded to 'decision' immediately throws open the problem of interpretation. In the first place, the study of power cannot ignore the perspectives of the allegedly relevant actors. The reason is straightforward. Their definitions of outcome may differ from the observer's and effectively locate them in a different process from the one the observer would place them in.

It may well be, of course, that false consciousness on the part of some actors makes such an injunction of dubious value. 'Indeed, is it not the supreme exercise of power to get another or others to have the desires you want them to have – that is, to secure their compliance by controlling their thoughts and desires?'[42] The question of false consciousness poses real difficulties since the only way of demonstrating that actor A suffers false consciousness is to appeal to some objective standard that others think that A would surely have followed had he been allowed. Since the standards to be applied are then likely to be as open to dispute as the original claim of false consciousness, nothing is resolved.[43] All the more reason that, in the second place, the observer's interpretation of the outcome, and of the process in which it is believed to be located, is made explicit. The statement and illustration of the counterfactual require this. If it is not done, there is no way of judging the significance of recorded events, and no way of judging the relevance, or realism, of actors' perspectives. The study of power needs this dual approach to avoid the extremes of narrow focus (imputing too much power to individuals), and vagueness (locating power in some de-personalised structure).

5 Structure

The central problem in the study of power is the identification of relevant core elements, and, of these, 'outcome' is the critical focusing device. The previous chapter has shown how this, and the associated problem of counterfactual statement, present problems that are of immediate and specific consequence for the structuring of any power analysis. In a very obvious sense, how we organise data collection and presentation of evidence can be of major importance in shaping the conclusions reached. As a result of analysing research methods and findings in eighty-three community power studies 'from a sociology of knowledge perspective' James Curtis and John Petras point out the apparently close relationship between methodology and conclusions. Decision-making analysis is justified by pluralist structural premises and leads to pluralist conclusions; reputational analysis is justified by elitist structural premises and leads to elitist conclusions.[1] Structure is so much part of the way in which power is identified and discussed that no power study ignoring its requirements can be taken seriously. The question arises then: what are these requirements?

If we look at the way in which 'structure' has been dealt with in the two major contributions to the empirical study of community power, we can immediately see the difficulty that is presented. Consider first the case of Floyd Hunter's *Community Power Structure*. In this, Hunter demonstrates the activities of the members of a reputed elite going about their (power) business. At the heart of this elite activity is a fluid committee structure that 'assumes keystone importance. The committee as a structure is a vital part of community power relations in Regional City'.[2] In spite of this emphasis, Hunter's committee theory remains very much a 'black box theory'. We are not shown how any committee does in fact operate, and we are not shown how any plurality of them provides the continuity and interconnectedness implicit in the term 'structure'. Nevertheless, Hunter also has an abstract frame of reference which is 'put forward to guide the study of community power

70

structure'.[3] The most significant aspect of such a strategy is that it would seek to identify institutions, organisations and groups, and patterns of interaction within and between them. Hunter argues, in the fourth of his 'Postulates on Power Structure', that the 'power of the individual must be structured into associational, clique, or institutional patterns to be effective'.[4] It is here that his difficulty emerges. Hunter's emphasis throughout his study is on the actions of individuals. And in Postulate 4 he effectively reserves all power to the individual and treats the association, clique, or institution, as an enabling medium. But we would surely not want to deny that the association or institution may be powerful independently of the actions of its members. The discussion in Chapter 2 has shown how power may be attributed to a collectivity because of the effect of its image. In some cases, of course, the institution may be powerful because a powerful individual is behind it. It is probably more often the case, though, that the individual is powerful because he or she is part of a powerful institution. Because of this emphasis, Hunter makes the wider structure of 'associational, clique, or institutional patterns' subordinate to the actions of the identified members of the elite. We are left with the picture of a city where things happen for one of two reasons: either almost every man wills continuity; or the relatively few decide on change.[5] There may well be occasions on which those simple truths hold. But life is a bit more complicated than that. Hunter neglects the structure within which such action may occur. Structure is subordinate to agency.

By contrast, Robert Dahl's *Who Governs?* is regarded as an example of decisional, or issue, analysis. Nelson Polsby, closely involved with Dahl as a research assistant on the project, wrote that 'The major purpose of the study was to explain certain events . . . related to the making and execution of public policy',[6] and Dahl noted that his 'issue analysis' approach was 'intended to penetrate the veil of official position and overt participation in order to determine as far as possible, who *really* influences decisions'.[7] In view of this emphasis it is interesting to note that only 83 out of a total of 325 pages are given over to analysis of three issue areas – political nominations 1941–57; urban redevelopment 1950–9; and public education 1950–9 – covering a total of 37 years.[8] This is hardly a detailed study of interaction of the type called for by Dahl's definition of power.

The remainder of *Who Governs?*, following the analysis of the three issue areas, becomes an exercise in leader and subleader role analysis. Chapter 13 and 14 provide a brief description of role occupants, patterns of recruitment, and role specialisation. Chapters 15 to 18 present alternative patterns of leadership role adjustments. Chapters 19 to 26 try to find some basis, in resource distribution and resource utilisation, for the observed role pattern. The last two chapters, 27 and 28, consider the relationship between role potential and role enactment within the normative framework of American democracy.

So Dahl presents a very lengthy analysis of the way in which the roles of his hypothetical power actors, *A* and *B*, may be structured. As a background to a study of power it is thoroughgoing and informative. But it cannot be a substitute for the depiction of an actual relationship between *A* and *B* which, in Dahl's terms at least, is the only point at which relevant information can be collected. Even though Dahl's work is avowedly action-oriented – in the sense that is self-evidently implied by a study of decision-making – the emphasis is heavily towards the structural framework within which action supposedly takes place.

For both Dahl and Hunter, then, there is an unresolved tension between the demands of structure and agency. Lukes argues that this opposition is pervasive, and is typically resolved in one of three ways. The *voluntarist* emphasises the initiative of the individual, reducing structural constraint to the minimum. The *structuralist* adopts a deterministic stance and denies the significance of human agents. The *relativist* simply refuses to relate the two positions, arguing that there are just different points of view and there is no way to choose between them.[9]

Lukes argues that 'all three fail, in fact, to address the very problem at issue, namely, that of the relation between power and structure'[10] and it does seem that any attempt to address the problem lands up on one side or the other of this 'pervasive opposition'. Stewart Clegg's approach, for example, starts from a neo-Marxist position which places hegemonic dominance rooted in the mode of production at the centre of social reality. Against this overweening structure, 'One cannot choose what dominates one other than through concerted class praxis as a revolutionary way of reformulating dominance'.[11] This extraordinary vision of the struggling individual demonstrating the inadequacy of a determinist interpretation of his position by provoking 'concerted class praxis' highlights the air of unreality that quickly pervades any attempt to bridge the gap that is created by regarding structure and action as polar opposites. To be fair, Clegg's discussion is far more complex than this and tries to provide room for an individual who is not totally determined. He sees structure as generated at the level of hegemonic dominance which is manifested in ground rules. It is these that determine the 'mode of rationality' – specifically the 'sedimented selection rules' within which action is constrained and demonstrated by, for example, 'instances of organisation practice'.[12] He emphasises the priority of the mode of production, but notes that:

> In spheres other than those concerned with the institutional area of the economy, the level of domination is only contingently determined by the mode of production. This allows subjects considerably more choice, theoretically at the surface level of social practice and action. None the less, this freedom, as all freedom, is conditioned.[13]

In considering the recurring, sequential relationship between structure, mediation (i.e. 'mode of rationality') and action, therefore, Clegg accords priority to structure: 'the present moment of action . . . is always produced from a past moment of structural conjuncture . . . mediated through strategies'.[14] Yet power is defined as 'the ability to exercise control over resources which, when subjects engage in practices, produce effects on other subjects'.[15] Clegg illustrates the sort of thing he means by 'practice' by referring to 'the visible structure of social relations in the organisation, and changes in those relations'.[16] In other words, Clegg's response to the problem posed by Lukes, so far as this can be understood, is that power simply describes the potentialities and use of the 'floorspace' left relatively clear to the individuals ('subjects') after the 'ground rules', 'sedimented selection rules', and 'instances of organisation practice'[17] have established their claim – like stalls at a bring-and-buy sale. The relationship between this relatively clear space and the various obstacles is determined by the push and shove caused as objects are brought in and taken out. The bulkier the object (resource), the more the existing obstacles will get shoved around or displaced entirely.

If the analogy is at all relevant, the pertinent question to ask, of course, is 'Who organises the sale?'. Clegg emphasises the priority of structure in one breath, but then disposes of the principle in dealing with the problem of introducing an agent who is something more than a mere structural co-ordinate. Structure is the 'hegemonic domination of some "objective principle" which, in the last instance, will tend to be conditioned economically by the mode of production'.[18] He concludes his analysis by arguing that

> individual power relations are only the visible tip of a structure of control, hegemony, rule and domination which maintains its effectiveness not so much through overt action, as through its ability to appear to be *the* natural convention. It is only when control slips, assumptions fail, routines lapse and 'problems' appear that the overt exercise of power is necessary.[19]

If 'structure' is a tool that is created, maintained and altered for a specific purpose in the same way as Schattschneider's 'mobilisation of bias', we are forced to regard 'action as *foundational* for a concept of . . . structure'.[20] But this is a curious conclusion to reach since these are the words that Clegg uses to dismiss the approach of Anthony Giddens, and from which he proceeds to develop his own ideas.

Clegg tries to bridge the gap between two opposed principles. Giddens prefers to view them as analytically distinct features of an otherwise inseparable whole and emphasises such an approach. He argues that 'action' should not be seen as referring to 'a series of discrete acts combined together, but to a *continuous flow of conduct*'.[21] Action is therefore *essentially* present in any understanding of structure and one could argue that 'structure' is a way of establishing the relationship of any given action with any other action. So our definition of structure will be dependent on our understanding or interpretation of any given action, and will also be dependent on what action we choose to identify. Inevitably the concept of 'structure' is to be seen as subordinate in such an action-oriented approach. What part, though, does our idea of the structural importance of any given action have in the selection of that action? And are we to regard this idea of structure as distinct from the structure that is identified in action? Giddens argues that 'Structure enters into the explanation of action in a dual way: as the medium of its production and at the same time as its outcome in the reproduction of social forms'.[22] In other words, structure is both an agent and an outcome. Neither as agent nor as outcome, however, can it be identified, but only in the traces it leaves through the process of action.

This brief account of the positions taken by Clegg and Giddens suggests that they offer no ready solution to the problem of establishing the structural limits of power. They both point to the dangers of any simple opposition between the two concepts and emphasise their inter-penetration. Both, for example, see social structure as being not only constitutive, in the sense that it shapes actions, but also constituted in that it is also shaped in its turn. Similarly Stewart Ranson, Bob Hinings and Royston Greenwood, in discussing two approaches to the description of structure as formal configuration of roles and procedures, i.e. *framework*, and as patterned regularities and processes of *interaction*, cite various ways in which 'patterns of interaction are not prescribed by structural frameworks'. They refer to studies which demonstrate 'the possibility of members displacing goods, subverting roles, and amplifying rules' and which 'suggest that the "rational" panoply of roles, rules, and procedures which make up organisational design is not pregiven in the organisation but is the skilled, practical, and retrospective accomplishment of members'.[23] Yet this degree of fluidity has to be placed alongside observed continuity; 'stability is acknowledged'. They argue, therefore, that:

> The unhelpful contrasting of framework and interaction can be overcome by conceiving of structure as a complex medium of control which is continually produced and recreated in interaction and yet shapes that interaction: structures are constituted and constitutive.[24]

In other words, Ranson, Hinings and Greenwood continue to see structure and action as opposed principles, but recognise that the distinction is largely analytic. Lukes takes a similar approach. His view is of an expanding and contracting social universe, with power and structure referring to changing patterns of abilities and opportunities respectively, occasionally disturbed by a 'big bang' whenever structures are 'created, maintained and destroyed by acts of power',[25] or 'at certain periods of social transformation'.[26] In other words, change may be caused by agency or structure. This 'now-you-see-it-now-you-don't' approach no doubt has more than a grain of sense in it. Lukes is probably right to say that 'social life can only be properly understood as a dialectic of power and structure, a web of possibilities for agents, whose nature is both active and structured, to make choices and pursue strategies within given limits, which in consequence expand and contract over time'.[27] The problem is to know what to do with such an expansive claim. Certainly the examples that Lukes looks at by way of illustrating some of his points are so shapeless as to defy analysis of the sort advocated and developed here.[28]

By contrast with power (itself a slippery concept), structure seems to defy clarification of any sort. At least, this is how it seems from Lukes' treatment. Power is succinctly defined as 'the capacity to bring about consequences'.[29] This understanding of power is developed further, but the foundation for future discussion is made clear. Lukes' approach requires that power in society is to be understood by observing the behaviour of actors.[30] The prescription for the understanding of structure, however, seems to be much the same except that the indicator for the observer to watch for is actors' failure, or lack of capacity, to effect any consequences. Structure is seen as whatever sets limits to 'the power of agents within some assumed time period'.[31] We cannot understand 'structure' until we have seen power in action. Where power fails, there is structure.

Lukes does not develop any substantive view of 'structure', asserting that it 'variously connotes 'essence', 'totality', 'system of relationships', 'dependence of parts in relation to the whole', and then simply going on to note the uses to which the term has been put by a variety of eminent writers.[32] He believes that 'structural constraints limit the agent's freedom or power to act otherwise',[33] but notes elsewhere that 'views differ about what constitute structural factors, about what sort of limits they set upon agency and about whether the limits they set curtail freedom or provide the condition of its effective exercise'.[34] Since power is, presumably, one form of the effective exercise of freedom, structure can be seen as the condition rather than the negation of power. If structure is a prerequisite for power, it cannot be opposed to it. Lukes' exclusive emphasis on structure as constraint is, therefore, undermined. The attempt to assimilate a power/structure dichotomy to a free will/ determinist model comes unstuck, and Lukes' view of structure is no more substantial than the tide mark left by the rise and fall of power.

If the voluntarist–determinist debate is of no immediate relevance to the discussion of political power, how should the concept of 'structure' be approached? Note that there is an element of ambiguity in the use of the term thus far. It has been used to describe the approach of the observer (i.e. how did Dahl structure his observations?), as well as the nature of the thing being studied (i.e.

what was the structure of New Haven politics?). This ambiguity is at the heart of the term, but, rather than causing confusion, it offers a creative potential, as will be shown.

Raymond Boudon suggests that any attempt to understand the meaning of the term must 'investigate the role played by this concept in the contexts in which it appears'.[35] Lukes agrees with Boudon, taking him to mean that a 'structural analysis of some object is simply the theory of that object viewed as a system'.[36] This interpretation is inaccurate. Boudon explicitly distinguishes between 'intentional' and 'operative' definitions of structure. He argues that where:

> the concept of structure appears in the context of an intentional definition . . . [it] serves only to indicate that an object has been identified as a system . . . (but where) an operative definition is involved . . . the object-system is analysed by means of a theory comparable to those of the natural sciences. The structure of the object is nothing else than the description resulting from the application of such a theory.[37]

An 'intentional' definition of structure emphasises that structure is independent of the inquiring mind, and is present in the object studied regardless of the views of the observer. There may be many differing interpretations, but only one can be right. S. F. Nadel argues that:

> social structure of whatever degree of refinement . . . (is) . . . still the social reality itself, or an aspect of it, not the logic behind it; and I consider structural analysis to be no more than a descriptive method, however sophisticated, not a piece of explanation.[38]

The difficulty with such an approach is to know how to recognise what is 'right'. In the physical sciences, understanding equals enhanced prediction, but in the social sciences the gap between the two can be very wide because of the significance of unpredictability in human behaviour. Robert Dowse suggests that the response by social scientists to the intractability of the facts in the face of attempts at structural explanation has been:

> to zoom to a higher level of abstraction and charac-

terize . . . society as held together by a common value system –
a political structure – engendered and disseminated by schools,
media, parties and so on in a manner that contributes to
generalized satisfactions with political outcomes and, hence, the
status quo.[39]

On such a view structural determinism (which is logically entailed
by an 'intentional' definition of structure) is not refuted by 'trivial'
inconsistent behaviours since it is demonstrated at this more all-
embracing level by the maintenance of the *status quo*. But, as Dowse
notes, 'no-one has succeeded in detecting the presence of such value
systems in any considerable number of heads'.[40] The irony is, then,
that if structures do exist in the sense that is meant by Boudon's
'intentional' form, they are poorly structured.

Where an 'operative' definition of structure is adopted, the
crucial role of the observer is underlined. Such an argument
emphasises that structure is a product of mind used to organise
phenomena in a way that is, presumably, sympathetic to the
observer's values. In this view, according to Nadel, 'structure is an
explanatory construct meant to provide the key to the observed facts
of social existence, the principles or formulae accounting for its
reality'.[41] Claude Lévi-Strauss, for example, argues that 'the term
"social structure" has nothing to do with empirical reality but with
models which are built up after it'.[42] In other words, the extent to
which structure can shape any given action is a function of its
explanatory power. Our explanatory framework is created to fit the
facts, but also creates them. As David Easton puts it, 'a fact is a
particular ordering of reality in terms of a theoretical interest'.[43]
The immediate difficulty with such an approach is that the
structure so created can represent a barrier between the observer
and the observed so that the structured facts tell more about the
interests of the observer than they do about the experiences of the
observed.

Is there any way to decide which of these two interpretations of
structure is to be preferred as a means of enhancing a study of
power? Surely any attempt to make a choice would be very difficult
since there is no common ground on which such a debate could be
held. But help is at hand. There is, after all, no reason why both
points of view should not be held. The problem in each case does not
lie in the initial position, but in the lengths to which it is taken as a
sole guiding principle. The 'intentional' approach becomes identi-

fied with the reification of structure, and with the constrictions of the free will versus determinism debate – from which we are well saved.[44] The 'operative' approach leads to a separation of the thing that is to be explained (*explicandum*), and the thing by which it is to be explained (*explicans*). The *explicandum* is the process that is experienced, and the *explicans* is the structure of explanation. In the 'intentional' approach, structure becomes both. But we have to recognise, though, that two separate problems have been identified here.

The first problem concerns the cluttered mind that the observer brings to any recognition and analysis. Without some explicit attempt to organise this it can be apparent to neither the observer, nor anyone else, what the status of any conclusion is. Unless thought is structured, its conclusions can be no more than 'occult effects'[45] adorned with facts, and, as Popper points out, 'scientific knowledge . . . is concerned not with *questions of fact* . . . but only with questions of *justification or validity*'.[46]

The second problem concerns the coherence of the objects studied by social scientists. To claim that these have some internal coherence is not at all arbitrary. After all, any organising concept such as 'election', 'legislation', 'conflict', refers to purposive activity.[47] In other words, the objects of social scientific study are already meaningfully structured by the relevant electoral, legislative or conflicting actors themselves. It has already been argued above[48] that the social scientist cannot make that the only level of meaning that he is concerned with. But it is inconceivable that any observer should ignore it.

The consequences of this argument are straightforward, even if the detailed implications are not. In the first place we have to understand that it is not possible to ask questions about power without structural implications at two different levels of meaning – that of observer and observed.[49] So the consideration of 'structure' returns to precisely the point that was reached in the discussion of outcome. The nature of action cannot be understood if we ignore the perspectives of the participants, and these are best seen in terms of orientation to an outcome. And since no action by a reputed power actor can be conclusively demonstrated to have been necessary for the outcome identified, we must provide some counterfactual structure. The observer says, 'This is how I think things usually work', and contrasts this with an observed process whose boundaries are determined by actor orientation to outcome.

The second consequence of the argument developed here is that the logic behind the 'core elements' approach needs to be applied to both levels of meaning, to the elaboration of both forms of structure that have been identified. For example, the operative structure, by which the observer makes possible the testing of the counterfactual proposition, must elaborate the relevant statuses (actors) within the system, the typical roles (actions) performed by them, the manifest functions[50] (intentions) by reference to which the statuses and roles are identified, and the functional imperatives (outcomes) which justify the shape of the structure presented. It is not meant that status, role, manifest function and functional imperative are precisely equivalent to actors, actions, intentions and outcome. This is particularly the case for the relationship between manifest function and intention, but since a status cannot intend anything there cannot be any objection to the obvious gap between the two terms. Whatever equivalents are used, the observer has the responsibility for stating what he believes to be the typical way in which the core elements are thought to interact. This was an outstanding feature of Dahl's study of New Haven. What was missing was an elaboration of the appropriate outcome-structure, and this followed from Dahl's preoccupation with decision-making.

In discussing the value of 'structure' as a conceptual tool, Nadel argues that 'in the final analysis, its weaknesses seem greatly to outweigh its strength', and he goes on to ground this in the term's 'narrow compass' which makes it seem 'impossible to speak of social structure in the singular'.[51] But what Nadel identifies as the term's weakness is, in fact, its strength. And, in the present context, the lack of singularity that Nadel rightly identifies does not connote a limitless spread of possibilities but, quite simply, a duality that has been suggested here as an essential aspect of the application of the term to empirical analysis. If 'structure' creates problems for power analysis, they arise because the concept represents the point at which the perspectives of the observer and of the observed intersect. No study that ignores one of these can be regarded as adequate: no study that searches for one unitary structure can hope to embrace both.

6 Conclusion

Any criticism that might be made of the community power literature[1] must be countered by praise for the pioneering contribution of researchers such as Hunter, Dahl, Agger, Goldrich and Swanson, and Presthus. Lukes is no pioneer, but his brief exposition of the issues involved both revived and dramatised an otherwise flagging argument. The debate has its critics, but it is an important debate, and one that political scientists, at least, cannot afford to ignore. One point made clear by Lukes is that approaches to power typically carry an ideological commitment,[2] and that the radical is apt to make claims about the operation of power that are hardest to answer.

Suppose, for example, that we are concerned at the 'oppression' of the slum dweller, and, believing it impossible that anyone would choose to live under such conditions, look elsewhere for the cause of their condition. We would be foolish to believe that this can be traced to the exercise of power simply by demonstrating that Landlord Grab benefits. Rejecting that sort of interpretation offers no justification, though, for attributing their condition to 'force of circumstances', 'structural determination', or some other ghost in the machine. All of these may be relevant to an explanation, but they are not the only alternatives to Landlord Grab.

This is obviously a difficult question, and there is no reason why it should be made to look easy. The pluralist would steer clear of it because no relevant political issue has been debated in the decision-making arena. The neo-elitist[3] would look for covert acts – mainly those which have the effect of preventing access to the decision-making arena. The radical would throw the onus of proof on the definition of the slum dwellers' 'real' interests. But in each case what is missing is a statement of the condition that is to be explained. The pluralist and neo-elitist miss the mark because they start out with assumptions about the location of power that emphasise process at the expense of outcome. The 'radical' approach is not entirely off the mark, but it covers only part of what is required. The 'real' interests of actors may be relevant to a study of power, but equally they may not. For example, the notion of 'real' interest is useful for the purpose of establishing a counterfactual in a case where the observer believes that power has been exerted to prevent something happening. Although objections can then be raised that the interests so identified may be no more real than others that can be nominated, that does not amount to an objection in principle to the method. But in cases where a power analyst wants to explain something that has happened then it does not really matter whether the outcome was in someone's interests or against them. If the outcome can be shown to have been intended, and if we can reasonably show that it would not otherwise have occurred, then we have demonstrated that power was, in fact, exerted. In such a case the identification of interest is irrelevant.

Foreshortening the power perspective by erasing 'outcome' can have an insidious effect. It can concentrate attention on those aspects of a process that are more obviously under actor control. This criticism is particularly appropriate in relation to the elitist and pluralist approaches. The result is to place undue stress on the ubiquity of power, or at least of a particular type of power. But the value of any power study does not lie so much in the identification of a power actor, or the critical act of power, as in the understanding it gives us of the dynamics of a process. Nadel's discussion of the value of structural analysis is relevant here:

> Our gain lies in the application of the appropriate analytic methods, not in gathering together, schematically, the results. For it is in the course of this application that we achieve a penetrating insight into the working of society. Every step in the many abstractions and comparisons we have to make reveals crucial interdependencies . . . Above all, in progressively discounting the particular features of social situations (which is the essence of abstraction), we prepare the way for the discovery of general characteristics and regulations, and hence of the lawfulness – such lawfulness as obtains – in the realm of social existence.[4]

The 'core element' approach is concerned with identifying the general characteristics of power. This means that it is antagonistic towards the tendency to approach the discussion of power from the perspectives of a dyadic confrontation. The tendency to keep the discussion of power within such limited terms is very marked. Dahl's definition is a classic example. Albert Weale justified focusing 'on the measurement of power in simple unilateral power situations' by arguing that 'unless the conceptual problems are cleared up at this level, we shall never have anything approaching a reasonable account of the overall distribution of power within a society'.[5]

The implication of this emphasis is that the dyad is the fundamental building block for all further power studies for which one needs only additional data. Peter Abell notes that the dyad is 'convenient for expository purposes', though he recognises 'that the extension to the many actor case introduces a number of different conceptualisations'.[6] These approaches show a misunderstanding of the problem. 'Simple unilateral power situations', as Weale puts it, are simply not representative. A 'building block' theory of knowledge is valid only where the original and subsequent components are compatible. In the case of the dyad, though, we are offered the atypical as the foundation stone. The atypicality of the dyad is outlined by Simmel in the following terms:

> More generally speaking, the difference between the dyad and larger groups consists in the fact that the dyad has a different relation to each of its two elements than have larger groups to their members. Although, for the outsider, the group consisting of two may function as an autonomous, super-individual unit, it usually does not do so for its participants. Rather, each of the two feels himself confronted only by the other, not by a collectivity above him. The social structure here rests immediately on the one and on the other of the two, and the secession of either would destroy the whole. The dyad, therefore, does not attain the super-personal life which the individual feels to be independent of himself.[7]

On this view there is no point at all in taking the dyad as the point of departure in the study of power since it is just not representative of the type of relationship with which social scientists are typically concerned. The dyadic focus trivialises. The only way that power research can develop the sort of insights to which Nadel refers is by focusing on the core elements within the context of a framework established by identifying the outcome to be studied.

We have learnt little from community studies about the core elements of power. This applies in particular to 'outcome' and

'intention'. Statement of outcome is the key focusing device for any
study of power, whether it is a study of 'power as a resource' or of
'power as relation'. The observer has an obvious obligation to make
explicit what it is that he is interested in, as well as a responsibility to
avoid trivialising reality by arbitrarily foreclosing the scope of
enquiry. Community power studies have either not made clear
what outcome is the focus of study – leaving it, for example, at the
vague level of 'community power structure' or 'Who Governs?' –
or they have taken the fragment for the whole, focusing narrowly on
the decision-making process.

There is no difficulty in understanding what is involved in
specifying 'outcome', even though it may present considerable
problems in practical definition.[8] With 'intention' not only are
there obvious practical difficulties, illustrated in the discussion of
Agger, Goldrich and Swanson's reference to ideology and interests,
but there are considerable conceptual difficulties as well. These
disappear if we recognise that the concept should be heuristically
useful rather than analytically rigorous. Intentions are not always
consciously present in an actor's mind; they are as difficult to
determine in political life as they are in the courts of law and
therefore depend largely on contextual data. There is no short cut to
their identification, and no path to power without them. By limiting
discussion to the context of decision-making, power studies distort
and restrict any understanding. Mayor Lee, for example, certainly
intended that his urban redevelopment scheme should be approved.
But surely his intentions were more specifically grounded than that?

This lack of focus puts obstacles in the way of dealing with any
counterfactual statement. If we are not clear as to what condition is
being asserted, then we obviously cannot consider the possibilities of
its non-occurrence. Is this sheer pedantry? Surely, evidence that
Mayor Lee secured the redevelopment programme is enough to
show that he was powerful. The trouble, though, is that no evidence
in the social sciences can be wholly conclusive. Unless we explicitly
consider the validity of the counterfactual statement, we cannot say
that we have properly tested our hypothesis. The process of focusing
for the purpose of asking a question is necessarily a distortion. Dahl
distorted New Haven politics by putting Mayor Lee at the centre in
the way that he did – although whether this was a major or minor
distortion is not at question here. Certainly the outsider would have
been able to judge this to some extent if Dahl had provided an
adequate model of New Haven politics, and particularly if the

office, or role, of mayor had been explicitly included. The judgement would also have been clearer if the counterfactual had been considered. The effect of not doing so inflates the apparent scope of actor control because that is, quite simply, what we are then setting out to find. The corollary is that such an approach minimises the significance of unintended effects. Counterfactual argument does not have to be a phase of analysis to be entered upon when the main work is completed, just to see if our conclusions stand up. It is rather, to be seen as an attitude of scepticism to be adopted even towards our own pet theories. It is a further witness to the importance of method in the study of power.

Nowhere is the reference to method more appropriate than in structuring the observer's and subject's separate relationship to outcome. This problem of structure has not been handled particularly well in power studies. Hunter's 'Postulates on Power' represent an attempt to provide an 'operative' structure as a foil to the 'intentional' structure based upon information derived from his respondents. Neither is sufficiently well developed to serve as an adequate basis for a study of power. Dahl's approach was dominated by an elaborately conceptualised 'operative' role structure servicing the needs of the decision-making process. The meaning that politics may have had for his actors is not tested on this Procrustean bed. Dahl may argue that his model of New Haven politics does, in fact, reflect the views of the population. In most cases the observer will try to avoid disparities between his interpretation and that of his subjects. But the point of stressing the duality of structure is that such a view should not be taken for granted – at least within a democratic context.

When we look at the works of Presthus and of Agger, Goldrich and Swanson, we find that both are preoccupied with the identification of 'intentional' structures, or as Parry puts it more directly, with the 'citizens' perception of the political system'.[9] Presthus does not balance against this any particular view of the structure of politics in the communities he studied. His introductory discussion is vague and over-generalised, and is no more helpful than Hunter's brief 'Postulates on Power'. By this time, though, the elitist–pluralist war was well under way. Presthus can perhaps be interpreted as trying to adopt a neutralist stance by placing the onus upon the ideological dimension. Agger, Goldrich and Swanson also emphasise popular perceptions. Their attempt to establish the objective structure of the citizens' political universe is complemented by a rather well thought out typology of power structure,[10] but one which is limited by their extraordinarily restricted decision-making focus.

In none of these studies do we find that structural demands are adequately met. This is largely because the authors nowhere express in reasonably comprehensive form the outcome that was of interest to them. Failure to provide a focus is damaging for any power analysis. It is not suggested that any study of political phenomena should adopt the form outlined here. A functional analysis, Weber's 'provisional orientation', does not need the focal point that is provided by the definition of outcome. The objective of functional analysis is to describe a totality of ordered relationships. The power analyst who purports to explain power in these terms is engaging in functional analysis. It may well be that there is some ordered structure behind all power relationships, but that is no excuse for saying that power analysis may, therefore, be reduced to functional analysis. Power analysis must incorporate functional analysis as an orienting device, but the reverse is not true. The study of power poses twice the problems, but offers greater insights. The corollary is that the greater potentiality of power analysis is available only where the observer is alert to its demands. If the requirements of the core elements are not recognised, these demands cannot be met.

It should be apparent from the preceding discussion that the study of power is not the neat incision in the fabric of society that categorical definition would imply. Much more is involved; so much more that the process of definition formation is distinctly obstructive. The core element approach is less elegant, but more realistic.

End-notes

1. Introduction

1. Floyd Hunter, *Community Power Structure: A Study of Decision Makers* (New York: Anchor, 1963).
2. Robert A. Dahl, *Who Governs? Democracy and Power in an American City* (New Haven, Conn. and London: Yale University Press, 1961).
3. Peter Bachrach and Morton S. Baratz, *Power and Poverty: Theory and Practice* (New York: Oxford University Press, 1970), and Steven Lukes, *Power: A Radical View* (London: Macmillan, 1974).
4. See Hugh V. McLachlan, 'Is "power" an evaluative concept?', *British Journal of Sociology*, 32 (1981) pp. 392–410, and especially pp. 394–6, where he points out that there is no immediately obvious conceptual difference between the views of Dahl, Bachrach and Baratz, and Lukes.
5. G. William Domhoff, *Who Really Rules? New Haven and Community Power Re-examined* (Santa Monica, Cal.: Goodyear, 1978) p. 126.
6. Robert A. Dahl, 'Power', in David L. Sills (ed.), *International Encyclopedia of the Social Sciences* (New York: Macmillan and The Free Press, 1968), vol. XII, pp. 405–15, at p. 414.
7. Hunter, *Community Power Structure*, p. 2.
8. Robert A. Dahl, 'The concept of power', *Behavioural Science*, 2 (1957) pp. 201–15, at pp. 202–3.
9. Brief discussions can be found in R. J. Mokken and F. N. Stokman, 'Power and influence as political phenomena', in Brian Barry (ed.), *Power and Political Theory: Some European Perspectives* (London: Wiley, 1976) pp. 33–54, at pp. 39–40; and in Dennis H. Wrong, *Skeptical Sociology* (London: Heinemann, 1977) pp. 168–72.
10. The problem of the counterfactual is discussed in Chapter 4 below.
11. Hunter, *Community Power Structure*, p. 9.
12. Lincoln Allison, 'The nature of the concept of power', *European Journal of Political Research*, 2 (1974) pp. 131–42, at p. 136.
13. Frederick M. Frohock, 'The structure of "politics"', *American Political Science Review*, 72 (1978) pp. 859–69.
14. Ibid., p. 861.
15. Ibid., p. 861.
16. Ibid., p. 862.
17. Ibid., p. 863.
18. Ibid., p. 867.
19. Ibid., p. 867.
20. Ibid., p. 868.

21. D. M. White, 'The concept of power: semantic chaos or underlying consensus', paper prepared for delivery at the Moscow IPSA Conference, 12–18 August 1979, p. 13, and *The Concept of Power* (Morristown, N.J.: General Learning Press, 1976) p. 3. See also Patrick Dunleavy, 'An issue centred approach to the study of power', *Political Studies*, 24 (1976) pp. 423–34, at p. 423 where he notes that 'The problems of power are primarily methodological'. Floyd Hunter disagrees. In *Community Power Succession: Atlanta's Policy-Makers Revisited* (Chapel Hill: University of North Carolina, 1980), he writes 'I feel that very much more time has been spent in the past two decades on methodological discussion than has been necessary', p. xii.

22. Robert Presthus, *Men at the Top: A Study in Community Power* (New York: Oxford University Press, 1964) p. 4.

23. Robert E. Agger, Daniel Goldrich and Bert E. Swanson, *The Rulers and the Ruled: Political Power and Impotence in American Communities* (New York: Oxford University Press, 1964) p. 195.

24. Bachrach and Baratz, *Power and Poverty*, pp. 21 and 37.

25. Lukes, *Power*, p. 27.

26. This is not to say that a comprehensive listing of concepts thought to be essential to all the conceivable approaches to power might not be useful in some way. Such an exercise would seem to fall within what White describes as a 'lowest common denominator approach' to a 'synthetic quest for a properly embracing concept of power': *The Concept of a Power*, p. 16.

27. Robert Axelrod, *Conflict of Interest* (Chicago: Markham, 1970) pp. 5, 7 and 13, draws attention to two types of conflict. 'Conflictful behaviour' includes all overt actions or states such as fights, quarrels, strikes and war. His second category is 'conflict of preferences' which, in fact, contains two different types. 'Conflict of preferences' derives from subjective awareness of conflict by virtue of opposition between one's own preferred value position and another. 'Conflict of interests', on the other hand, may be defined objectively without reference to the consciousness of the subject.

28. Robert A. Dahl, *Modern Political Analysis*, 2nd ed. (Englewood Cliffs, N.J.: Prentice Hall, 1970) p. 59.

29. Brian Barry, 'The economic approach to the analysis of power and conflict', *Government and Opposition*, 9 (1974) pp. 189–223, p. 198.

30. Jack H. Nagel, *The Descriptive Analysis of Power* (New Haven, Conn. and London: Yale University Press, 1975) p. 154.

31. See note on 'conflict' to Table 1.1.

32. See for example Talcott Parsons, 'Voting: and the equilibrium of the American political system', in Eugene Burdick and Arthur Brodbeck (eds), *American Voting Behaviour* (Glencoe, Ill.: The Free Press, 1959) pp. 80–120, at p. 81; Jan-Erik Lane, 'On the use of the word "political"', in Barry (ed.), *Power*, pp. 217–44, at p. 223; Anthony Giddens, *New Rules of Sociological Method* (London: Hutchinson, 1976) p. 112; Anthony de Crespigny, 'Power and its forms', *Political Studies*, 16 (1968) pp. 192–205, at p. 193; Felix E. Oppenheim, '"Power" Revisited', *Journal of Politics*, 40 (1978) pp. 589–608, at p. 607; Frederick W. Frey, 'Comment on issues and nonissues in the study of power', *American Political Science Review*, 65 (1971) pp. 1081–1101, at p. 1089.

33. See for example Albert Weale, 'Power inequalities', *Theory and Decision*, 7 (1976) pp. 297–313, at p. 306; David Easton, *The Political System* (New York:

Knopf, 1953) p. 144; Peter M. Blau, *Exchange and Power in Social Life* (New York: Wiley, 1964) p. 117; Robert Bierstedt, 'An analysis of social power', *American Sociological Review*, 15 (1950) pp. 730–8, at p. 733; Harold D. Lasswell and Abraham Kaplan, *Power and Society* (New Haven, Conn.: Yale University Press, 1950) p. 76.

34. For brief references see Allan Jones, 'Power politics', in David V. Edwards, *International Political Analysis: Readings* (New York: Holt, Rinehart and Winston, 1970) pp. 207–25, at p. 221; Mokken and Stokman, 'Power' pp. 33–54, point to the bias in such definitions, p. 35; and a more detailed discussion of this can be found in Arnold A. Rogow and Harold D. Lasswell, *Power, Corruption and Rectitude* (Westport, Conn.: Greenwood, 1963), Chapter 1, 'The tradition: power corrupts'. See also Rollo May, *Power and Innocence: A Search for the Sources of Violence* (London: Souvenir, 1974) pp. 100–101. Parry and Morriss point out that 'there is another way of looking at politics which lays far less stress on conflict and its resolution through decisive action . . . politics is the application of fairly standard procedures to recurrent problems rather than the settlement of "world-historical" conflict.' Geraint Parry and Peter Morriss, 'When is a decision not a decision?', in Ivor Crewe (ed.), *British Political Sociology Yearbook*, vol. 1 (London: Croom Helm, 1974) pp. 317–36, at pp. 320–1; see also Peter Nicholson, 'What is politics: determining the scope of political science', *Il Politico*, 42 (1977) pp. 228–49, at p. 232.

35. For example, see Herbert Simon, *Models of Man, Social and Rational* (New York: Wiley, 1957) p. 5; J. A. A. Van Doorn, 'Sociology and the problem of power', *Sociologia Neerlandica*, 1 (1962–3) pp. 3–51, at p. 12; Stanley Benn, 'Power', *The Encyclopaedia of Philosophy*, vi (London: Collier-Macmillan, 1967) p. 426; R. H. Tawney, *Equality* (London: George Allen & Unwin, 1931) pp. 175–6; Mokken and Stokman, 'Power', p. 49; Wrong, *Skeptical Sociology* p. 164; David V. J. Bell, *Power, Influence and Authority: An Essay in Political Linguistics* (New York: Oxford University Press, 1975) p. 21; Alfred Kuhn, *The Study of Society: A Unified Approach* (Homewood, Ill.: Irwin, 1963) p. 317. Sik Hung Ng, however interprets Dahl differently: 'The overcoming of resistance if necessary . . . becomes in effect the primary and exclusive element of Dahl's definition'; *The Social Psychology of Power* (London: Academic Press, 1980) p. 104.

36. For example, see T. V. Smith, 'Power: its ubiquity and legitimacy', *American Political Science Review*, 45 (1951) pp. 693–702, at p. 693; Bertrand Russell, *Power: A New Social Analysis* (London: George Allen & Unwin, 1938) p. 35; Talcott Parsons, *Structure and Process in Modern Society* (New York: The Free Press, 1960) p. 181; Quentin Gibson, 'Power', *Philosophy of the Social Sciences*, 1 (1971) pp. 101–12, at p. 107; Jon Elster, *Logic and Society: Contradictions and Possible Worlds* (Chichester: Wiley, 1978), p. 7; G. E. C. Catlin, *The Principles of Politics* (London: George Allen & Unwin, 1930) p. 154; Nagel, *Power*, p. 29.

37. Knut Midgaard 'Cooperative negotiations and bargaining: some notes on power and powerlessness', in Barry, *Power*, pp. 117–37, at p. 136; Mary Parker Follett, *Dynamic Administration* (London: Management Publications Trust Ltd, 1934) cited in Dorothy Emmett, 'The concept of power', *Proceedings of the Aristotelian Society*, new series 54, (1953–4) pp. 1–26, at p. 9; Hannah Arendt, *On Violence* (London: Allen Lane, 1970) cited in Lukes, *Power*, at p. 28.

38. R. G. Collingwood, *The New Leviathan* (Oxford: Clarendon, 1942) pp. 153–4.

The power of co-operative behaviour is also illustrated by P. H. Partridge, 'Some notes on the concept of power', *Political Studies*, 11 (1963) pp. 107–25, at p. 123.

39. Nagel, *Power*, p. 156.
40. Nagel, *Power*, p. 154.
41. The discussion of 'sanctions' and 'rational perception' (pp. 17–18) are taken from this author's 'Nondecisions and power: the two faces of Bachrach and Baratz', *American Political Science Review*, 69 (1975) pp. 889–99.
42. Bachrach and Baratz, *Power and Poverty*, p. 37.
43. Ibid., pp. 30–1.
44. Ibid., pp. 32–6.
45. Ibid., p. 37.
46. Peter Bachrach and Morton S. Baratz, 'Power and its two faces revisited: a reply to Geoffrey Debnam', *American Political Science Review*, 69 (1975) pp. 900–904, at p. 903.
47. Dahl, *Modern Political Analysis*, pp. 32–3.
48. de Crespigny, 'Power', p. 193.
49. Wrong, *Skeptical Sociology*; p. 167.
50. Mokken and Stokman, 'Power', pp. 33–54, at p. 39.
51. Ibid., p. 40.
52. Wrong, *Skeptical Sociology*, p. 169.
53. Carl J. Friedrich, *Constitutional Government and Democracy: Theory and Practice in Europe and America* (Boston, Mass.: Ginn, 1946) p. 589.
54. Arnold M. Rose, *The Power Structure: Political Processes in American Society* (New York: Oxford University Press, 1967) p. 47.
55. Brian Barry, 'Power: An Economic Analysis', in Barry, *Power*, pp. 67–101, at p. 71.
56. As Ball puts it, 'In the case of human agents, the explanatory *can* need not entail the predictive *will*'. Terence Ball, 'Power, causation and explanation', *Polity*, 8 (1975–6) pp. 189–214, at p. 214.
57. Nelson W. Polsby, *Community Power and Political Theory* (New Haven, Conn. and London: Yale University Press, 1980) p. 131.
58. Bachrach and Baratz, *Power and Poverty*, pp. 22 and 34.
59. Ibid., p. 30.
60. Ibid., p. 31.
61. Ibid., p. 19.
62. White writes in favour of a 'sufficient conditions approach . . . (that) allows for concentration on partial aspects of power without the generality of the matter being obscured', 'Concept of power', p. 17.

2. Actors and Action

1. Robert E. Agger, David Goldrich and Bert E. Swanson *The Rulers and the Ruled: Power and Impotence in American Communities* (New York: Oxford University Press, 1964) p. 10.
2. Floyd Hunter, *Community Power Structure* (New York: Anchor, 1963) pp. 5–6.
3. Steven Lukes, *Power: A Radical View* (London: Macmillan, 1974) p. 3.
4. Ibid., p. 52.

5. Ibid., p. 22.
6. Alan Bradshaw, 'A critique of Steven Lukes' "Power: A Radical View"', *Sociology*, 10 (1976) pp. 121–7, at p. 125.
7. Steven Lukes, 'Reply to Bradshaw', *Sociology*, 10 (1976) pp. 129–32, at p. 131.
8. Lukes, 'Reply to Bradshaw', p. 131.
9. Bob Jessop, 'On the commensurability of power and structural constraint', paper presented to the EGOS Symposium on Power, University of Bradford, 6–7 May 1976, p. 11.
10. Stewart Clegg, *The Theory of Power and Organization* (London: Routledge & Kegan Paul, 1979) pp. 57–64; Graham Cox, 'Intentions, structures and the dissolution of "Power"?', paper presented to the EGOS Symposium on Power, University of Bradford, 6–7 May 1976, p. 5; Bradshaw, 'A Critique of Lukes', p. 125.
11. See, for example, David Butler and Donald Stokes, *Political Change in Britain: The Evolution of Electoral Choice*, 2nd ed.(London: Macmillan, 1974) Chapter 16, 'Images of the parties'.
12. Max Weber, *The Theory of Social and Economic Organization* (New York: The Free Press, 1954) p. 102.
13. I. C. Jarvie, *Universities and Left Review* (1958–9) p. 57, cited in Steven Lukes, *Essays in Social Theory* (New York: Columbia University Press, 1977) p. 180.
14. Lukes, *Essays*, p. 180.
15. Ibid., p. 80.
16. Joseph Agassi, 'Methodological individualism', *British Journal of Sociology*, II (1960) pp. 244–70; J. O. Wisdom, 'Situational individualism and the emergent group properties', in Robert Borger and Frank Cioffi, *Explanation in the Behavioural Sciences* (London: Cambridge University Press, 1970) pp. 271–96.
17. Wisdom, 'Situational individualism', p. 274.
18. This argument is developed by S. J. Stoljar, *Groups and Entities: An Inquiry into Corporate Theory* (Canberra: Australian National University Press, 1973) p. 189.
19. See F. A. Hayek, *Studies in Philosophy, Politics and Economics* (London: Routledge & Kegan Paul, 1967) p. 100; K. R. Popper, *The Open Society and its Enemies*, vol. II (London: Routledge & Kegan Paul, 1966) pp. 94–5.
20. For criticism of Hayek on this point see Norman P. Barry, *Hayek's Social and Economic Philosophy* (London: Macmillan, 1979) p. 37. Partridge reminds us, though, that 'a realistic or adequate study of political or social power cannot afford to discount unintended effects'. P. H. Partridge, 'Some notes on the concept of power', *Political Studies*, 11 (1963) pp. 107–25, at p. 114.
21. Hunter, *Community Power Structure*, p. 222; and Robert A. Dahl, *Who Governs? Democracy and Power in an American City* (New Haven, Conn. and London: Yale University Press, 1961) pp. 332–3.
22. Agger, Goldrich and Swanson, *Rulers and the Ruled*, p. 47.
23. Ibid., p. 115.
24. John Stuart Mill, *Utilitarianism, Liberty and Representative Government* (London: Dent, 1910) pp. 151–2.
25. G. W. Jones, *Responsibility and Government* (London: London School of Economics, 1977) p. 3.
26. Agger, Goldrich and Swanson, *Rulers and the Ruled*, p. 13.

27. Peter Bachrach and Morton S. Baratz, *Power and Poverty: Theory and Practice* (New York: Oxford University Press, 1970) p. 44.
28. Ibid., p. 44.
29. Geraint Parry and Peter Morriss, 'When is a decision not a decision? ', in Ivor Crewe (ed.) *British Political Sociology Yearbook*, vol. 1 (London: Croom Helm, 1974) pp. 317–36, at p. 326.
30. Bachrach and Baratz, *Power and Poverty*, p. 45.
31. E. E. Schattschneider, *The Semi-Sovereign People: A Realist's View of Democracy in America* (New York: Holt, Rinehart and Winston, 1960) p. 71.
32. Peter Bachrach and Morton S. Baratz, 'Power and its Two Faces Revisited: A Reply to Geoffrey Debnam', *American Political Science Review*, 69 (1975) pp. 900–904, at p. 902.
33. Peter Bachrach and Morton S. Baratz, 'Decisions and nondecisions: an analytical framework', *American Political Science Review*, 57 (1963) pp. 632–42, at p. 641. This passage was omitted when the article was reprinted in Bachrach and Baratz, *Power and Poverty*.
34. Peter Bachrach and Morton S. Baratz, 'Letter to the Editor', *American Political Science Review*, 62 (1968) pp. 1268–9, at p. 1268.
35. Bachrach and Baratz, *Power and Poverty*, p. 8.
36. Dahl, for example, argues that 'Unless there is some "connection" between *A* and *a*, then no power relation can be said to exist. I shall leave the concept of "connection" undefined . . . '. See Robert A. Dahl, 'The concept of power', *Behavioral Science*, 2 (1957) pp. 201–15, at p. 204.
37. Bachrach and Baratz, 'Power and its Two Faces', p. 904.
38. Ibid., p. 904.
39. Bachrach and Baratz, *Power and Poverty*, p. 7.
40. See, for example, Nelson W. Polsby, 'Empirical investigation of mobilization of bias in community power research', *Political Studies*, 27 (1979) pp. 527–41, at p. 535.
41. Matthew A. Crenson, *The Un-Politics of Air Pollution: A Study of Non-Decisionmaking in the Cities* (Baltimore, Md and London: Johns Hopkins Press, 1971) p. 78.
42. Ibid., p. 69.
43. Edward Greer, 'Air pollution and corporate power: municipal reform limits in a black city', *Politics and Society* 4 (1974) 483–510, at p. 493.
44. Crenson, *Un-Politics*, p. 69.
45. John Gaventa, *Power and Powerlessness: Quiescence and Rebellion in an Appalachian Valley* (Oxford: Clarendon, 1980).
46. Ibid., p. 242.
47. This is a point that is central to the critique of Dahl's study of New Haven elaborated by William G. Domhoff, *Who Really Rules? New Haven and Community Power Reexamined* (Santa Monica, Cal.: Goodyear, 1969).
48. See Raymond E. Wolfinger, 'Nondecisions and the study of local politics', *American Political Science Review*, 65 (1977) pp. 1068–80, at p. 1077, where he asks 'Do we attribute power to John Dewey for his continuous influence in American education?' The answer is 'yes' as long as we can isolate the appropriate elements.
49. Lukes, *Power*, p. 50.
50. Ibid., p. 50.

51. Terence Ball, 'Power, causation and explanation', *Polity*, 8 (1975–6) pp. 189–214, at p. 190.
52. Ibid., p. 196.
53. Richard M. Merelman, 'Reply to "Comment" by Bachrach and Baratz', *American Political Science Review*, 62 (1968) pp. 1269.
54. Weber, *Theory of Social and Economic Organization*, p. 103.
55. Lukes, *Power*, p. 51.
56. Bradshaw, 'A Critique', p. 124.
57. Lukes, *Power*, p. 51.
58. Ibid., p. 51.
59. Dahl, 'The concept of power', p. 205.
60. de Crespigny, 'Power'. *Political Studies*, 16 (1968) pp. 192–205, at p. 194. See also P. H. Partridge, 'Some notes on the concept of power', *Political Studies*, 11 (1962) pp. 107–25, at p. 114; Ball, 'Power', p. 205; and Gibson Burrell and Gareth Morgan, *Sociological Paradigms and Organisational Analysis* (London: Heinemann, 1979) p. 215, who use the term 'negative power' to refer to 'the ability to stop things being done', which is a curious and unhelpful usage.
61. Lukes, *Power*, p. 52.
62. de Crespigny, 'Power', p. 193.
63. Parry and Morriss, 'When is a Decision not a Decision?', p. 331.
64. Hunter, *Community Power Structure*, p. 151.
65. See notes 36 and 48 above.

3. Intention

1. See, for example, Dennis Wrong, *Skeptical Sociology* (London: Heinemann) p. 166; Stanley Benn, 'Power', in Paul Edwards (ed.), *Encyclopedia of Philosophy* (New York: Macmillan and The Free Press, 1967) vol. vi, pp. 424–7, at p. 426; Bertrand Russell, *Power: A New Social Analysis* (London: George Allen & Unwin, 1938) p. 35; Terence Ball, 'Power, causation and explanation', *Polity*, 8 (1975) pp. 189–214, at p. 211; P. H. Partridge, 'Some notes on the concept of power', *Political Studies*, 11 (1962) pp. 107–25, at pp. 113–15; Anthony de Crespigny, 'Power and its forms', *Political Studies*, 16 (1968) pp. 192–205, at p. 192.
2. Lincoln Allison, 'The nature of the concept of power', *European Journal of Political Research*, 2 (1974) pp. 131–42 at p. 137.
3. Jack H. Nagel, *The Descriptive Analysis of Power* (New Haven, Conn. and London: Yale University Press, 1975) p. 20.
4. D. M. White, 'Power and intentions', *American Political Science Review*, 65 (1971) pp. 749–59, at p. 749.
5. White, 'Power', p. 752.
6. Robert K. Merton, 'The unanticipated consequences of social action', in Robert K. Merton, *Sociological Ambivalence and Other Essays* (New York: The Free Press, 1976) pp. 145–55, at p. 147.
7. Anthony Giddens, *New Rules of Sociological Method* (London: Hutchinson, 1976) p. 76. See also Stuart Hampshire, *Thought and Action* (London: Chatto & Windus, 1959) p. 72, where he writes, 'Sometimes I may admit that I have forgotten, not only what I was doing a few minutes ago, but even what I am

doing at this moment. In such a case I know that my present actions, narrowly defined, are in intention continuous with the actions that preceded them in such a way as to constitute a single continuous action.'

8. The argument in this and the next paragraph is based upon Graham Hughes, 'Criminal responsibility', *Stanford Law Review*, 16 (1964) pp. 470–85. The jurists cited by Hughes in this connection (p. 470) are J. W. Cecil Turner and Glanville Williams.

9. H. L. A. Hart, P. H. Nowell-Smith, Peter Brett, cited in Hughes, 'Criminal responsibility', pp. 471–72.

10. The view of Glanville Williams is that 'The test of negligence in terms of the reasonable man is called an "objective" standard, because it does not depend upon a finding of what passes in the defendant's mind . . . *Homo juridicus* is the ideal man, the moral man, the conscientious man – not setting the standard so high that life becomes impossible in ordinary terms, but nevertheless requiring the most careful consideration to be given, so-that harm is avoided and the law obeyed', *Textbook of Criminal Law* (London: Stevens, 1978) p. 43.

11. Nagel, *Descriptive Analysis of Power*, p. 20.

12. Stewart Clegg, 'Power, theorizing and nihilism', *Theory and Society*, 3 (1976) pp. 65–87, at p. 78.

13. Petro Georgiou, 'The concept of power: a critique and an alternative', *Australian Journal of Politics and History*, 23 (1977) pp. 252–67, at p. 262.

14. John R. Champlin, 'On the study of power', *Politics and Society*, 1 (1970) pp. 91'–111, at p. 93.

15. Clegg, 'Power, theorizing and nihilism', p. 78.

16. Merton, 'The unanticipated consequences', p. 148.

17. Nagel, *The Descriptive Analysis of Power*, p. 20. Although Nagel is wrong in his conclusions, he is right to point up the difficulties. Williams writes that, 'The two main forms of *mens rea* – intention (including knowledge) and recklessness – need further study . . . It is strange that, after more than a thousand years of continuous legal development, English law should still lack a clear definition of such important words as these. The general legal opinion is that "intention" cannot be satisfactorily defined, and does not need a definition, since everyone knows what it means.' Williams, *Textbook of Criminal Law*, p. 51.

18. Alasdair MacIntyre, 'A mistake about causality in social science', in *Philosophy, Politics and Society*, 2nd series, Peter Laslett and W. G. Runciman, (eds) (Oxford: Blackwell, 1969) pp. 48–70, at p. 58.

19. Ludwig Wittgenstein, *Philosophical Investigations* (New York: Macmillan, 1968) para 337, cited in John G. Gunnell, 'Political theory and the theory of action', in *The Western Political Quarterly*, 34 (1981) pp. 341–58, at p. 355.

20. Quentin Gibson, 'Power', *Philosophy of the Social Sciences*, 1 (1971) pp. 101–112, at p. 103.

21. Ibid., pp. 103–104.

22. See D. M. White, *The Concept of Power* (Morristown, N. J.: General Learning Press, 1976) p. 12.

23. Gibson, 'Power', and see Terence Ball, 'Power, causation and explanation', *Polity*, 8 (1975–6) pp. 189–214.

24. Gibson, 'Power', p. 105.

25. Ibid., p. 106.

26. Ibid., p. 103.

27. G. E. M. Anscombe, *Intentions* (Oxford: Blackwell, 1957) pp. 38–40, cited in John Meiland, 'Unintentional Actions', *Philosophical Review*, 72 (1963) pp. 377–81, at p. 381. A parallel example would be the case of the driver running into and killing a pedestrian. If this had been a deliberate action, he would have committed murder. Without such an intention the outward aspect remains the same, but the action is not murder.

28. White, 'Power and Intentions', p. 758.

29. Ibid., p. 759.

30. Ibid., p. 756.

31. Ibid., p. 756.

32. Ibid., p. 759.

33. Ibid., p. 750.

34. Robert Brown, *Explanation in Social Science* (London: Routledge & Kegan Paul, 1963) p. 74.

35. Ibid., p. 73.

36. Benjamin Azkin, 'On conjecture in political science', *Political Studies*, 14 (1966) pp. 1–14, at p. 14.

37. Floyd Hunter, *Community Power Structure: A Study of Decision Makers* (New York: Anchor, 1963) pp. 236–7.

38. Ibid., p. 237.

39. Ibid., p. 241.

40. Ibid., p. 146.

41. Ibid., p. 151.

42. Robert E. Agger, Daniel Goldrich and Bert E. Swanson, *The Rulers and the Ruled: Political Power and Impotence in American Communities* (New York: Oxford University Press, 1964) p. 61.

43. All citations in this paragraph are taken from Agger, Goldrich and Swanson, *The Rulers and the Ruled*, pp. 17 and 18.

44. Ibid., p. 17.

45. 'A letter concerning toleration', p. 126 in John Locke, *The Second Treatise of Civil Government and A Letter Concerning Toleration*, ed. with an Introduction by J. W. Gough (Oxford: Blackwell, 1948).

46. H. L. A. Hart, *Punishment and Responsibility: Essays in the Philosophy of Law* (Oxford: Clarendon Press, 1968) p. 121.

47. Both references are to the Editor's footnote to Max Weber, *The Theory of Social and Economic Organization*, ed. with an Introduction by Talcott Parsons (New York: The Free Press, 1964) p. 94.

48. Agger, Goldrich and Swanson, *The Rulers and The Ruled*, p. 5. See also the typology developed by C. Kadushin, 'Power, influence and social circles: a new methodology for studying opinion makers', *American Sociological Review*, 33 (1968) pp. 685–99.

49. See Robert A. Dahl, *Who Governs? Democracy and Power in an American City* (New Haven, Conn. and London: Yale University Press, 1961) p. 33; and Nelson W. Polsby, *Community Power and Political Theory*, (New Haven, Conn. and London: Yale University Press, 1963) pp. 112–21.

50. Terence Ball, 'Models of power: past and present', *Journal of the History of the Behavioural Sciences*, 11 (1975) pp. 211–22, at p. 216.

51. Weber, *Theory of Social and Economic Organization*, pp. 95–6.

52. Brown, *Explanation*, pp. 72–3.
53. On the problem of the historical analysis of power see John A. Garrard, 'The history of local political power – some suggestions for analysis', *Political Studies*, 25 (1977) pp. 252–69; and David C. Hammack, 'Problems in the historical study of power in the cities and towns of the United States, 1800–1960', *American Historical Review*, 83 (1978) pp. 323–49.

4. Outcome

1. J. A. A. Van Doorn, 'Sociology and the problem of power', *Sociologica Neerlandica*, 1 (1962–3) pp. 3–51, at p. 8.
2. Floyd Hunter, *Community Power Structure: A Study of Decision Makers* (New York: Anchor, 1963) pp. 170–2.
3. Ibid., pp. 211–15.
4. Robert Dahl, *Who Governs? Democracy and Power in an American City* (New Haven, Conn. and London: Yale University Press, 1961) p. 120.
5. Ibid., p. 121.
6. Peter Bachrach and Morton S. Baratz, *Power and Poverty: Theory and Practice* (New York: Oxford University Press, 1970) p. 50.
7. See Dahl, *Who Governs?*, pp. 332–3.
8. Bachrach and Baratz, *Power and Poverty*, p. 62.
9. Steven Lukes, *Power: A Radical View* (London: Macmillan, 1974) pp. 16–20.
10. Ibid., p. 27.
11. Ibid., p. 26.
12. D. M. White, 'The problem of power', in *British Journal of Political Science*, 2 (1972) pp. 479–90, at p. 488.
13. Ibid., p. 483.
14. See discussion of conflict in Chapter 1 above.
15. See reference under note 6 above.
16. Nelson W. Polsby, *Community Power and Political Theory: A Further Look at Problems of Evidence and Inference*, 2nd ed. (New Haven, Conn. and London: Yale University Press, 1980) p. 132.
17. Allen Schick, 'Systems politics and systems budgeting', *Public Administration Review*, 29 (1969) pp. 137–51, at p. 138.
18. Michael Parenti, *Power and the Powerless* (New York: St Martin's Press, 1978) pp. 32–3. See also Patrick Dunleavy, 'An issue centred approach to the study of power', *Political Studies*, 24 (1976) pp. 423–34, at p. 427, where he notes that 'pluralist researchers were content simply to attack the conclusions of reputational studies, and they downgraded outputs to the level where they were barely mentioned, contravening the basic methodology outlined by Polsby'.
19. Polsby, *Community Power*, 2nd ed., p. 209.
20. Ibid., p. 218. For reference to Bachrach and Baratz's circumlocutions on the theme see pp. 31–4 above. Matthew Crenson's orientation can be found in *The Un-Politics of Air Pollution: A Study of Non-Decisionmaking in the Cities* (Baltimore, Md and London: Johns Hopkins Press, 1971) pp. 23–6.
21. Frank Levy, Arnold J. Meltsner and Aaron Wildavsky, *Urban Outcomes: Schools, Streets and Libraries* (Berkeley, Cal.: University of California Press,

1974) pp. 2 and 7; and see Jeanne Becquart-Leclercq, 'French mayors and communal policy outputs: the case of small cities', in Roland J. Liebert and Allen W. Imersheim, *Power Paradigms and Community Research* (London and California: Sage, 1977) pp. 79–119, at p. 113, where she notes that the 'concept of *outcomes* refers to the social impact of outputs'.

22. But see Yehezkel Dror, *Public Policymaking Reexamined* (Scranton, Penn.: Chandler, 1968) pp. 34–5 for an acknowledgement of the obstacles to such clear judgements in real life situations.

23. Lukes, *Power*, p. 41.

24. Karl R. Popper, *The Logic of Scientific Discovery* (London: Hutchinson, 1972) Chapter 4.

25. Jon Elster, 'The treatment of counterfactuals: reply to Brian Barry', in *Political Studies*, 28 (1980) pp. 144–7, at p. 145.

26. Fuller references to Crenson's study can be found at p. 27 and at pp. 62–5.

27. Dahl, *Who Governs?*, pp. 120–21.

28. Brian Barry, 'Superfox', *Political Studies*, 28 (1980) pp. 136–43, at p. 140. Elster points out, however, that although we do not require a full-blooded alternative world, we must have 'a skeleton world, a configuration of values of some finite set of variables'. See his 'Reply to comments', *Inquiry*, 23 (1980) pp. 213–32, at p. 221.

29. Dahl, *Who Governs?*, pp. 115–18.

30. R. A. Young, 'Steven Lukes's radical view of power', *Canadian Journal of Political Science*, 11 (1978) pp. 639–49, at p. 641. Geraint Parry and Peter Morriss, 'When is a decision not a decision?' in Ivor Crewe (ed.), *British Political Sociology Yearbook*, vol. 1 (London: Croom Helm, 1974) pp. 313–37, at p. 331 point out more reasonably that 'it is difficult to ensure comparability'.

31. Lukes, *Power*, p. 45.

32. Crenson, *The Un-Politics of Air Pollution*, pp. 35–82.

33. Ibid., p. 28.

34. Ibid., p. 40.

35. Ibid., p. 40.

36. Ibid., p. 78.

37. Ibid., pp. 80–1.

38. For K. Newton's review of Crenson's book see 'Democracy, community power and decision-making', *Political Studies*, 20 (1972) pp. 484–7; and for Polsby's comments see Nelson W. Polsby, 'Community power meets air pollution', *Contemporary Sociology*, 1 (1972) pp. 99–101, at p. 101; and in 'Empirical investigation of the mobilization of bias in community power research', *Political Studies*, 27 (1979) pp. 527–41, at p. 540; and yet again in *Community Power and Political Theory*, 2nd ed., p. 216.

39. John Gaventa, *Power and Powerlessness: Quiescence and Rebellion in an Appalachian Valley* (Oxford: Clarendon Press, 1980).

40. Ibid., p. 3.

41. Ibid. District 19 is dealt with in Chapter 7, and all other references appear in Chapter 2.

42. Lukes, *Power*, p. 23.

43. The literature on false consciousness and alienation is enormous. Recent contributions that are of close interest to the debate over power include Isaac

D. Balbus, 'The concept of interest in pluralist and Marxian analysis', *Politics and Society*, 1 (1971) pp. 151–77; Nicholas Abercrombie and Bryan S. Turner, 'The dominant ideology thesis', *British Journal of Sociology*, 29 (1978) pp. 149–70; Kenneth Prandy, 'Alienation and interest in the analysis of social cognitions', *British Journal of Sociology*, 30 (1979) pp. 442–74; and G. W. Smith, 'Must radicals be Marxists? Lukes on power, contestability and alienation', *British Journal of Political Science*, 11 (1981) pp. 405–25.

5. Structure

1. James E. Curtis and John W. Petras, 'Community power, power studies and the sociology of knowledge', *Human Organization*, 29 (1970) pp. 204–18.
2. Floyd Hunter, *Community Power Structure: A Study of Decision Makers* (New York: Anchor, 1963) p. 89.
3. Ibid., p. 5.
4. Ibid., p. 6.
5. Ibid., p. 10.
6. Nelson W. Polsby, *Community Power and Political Theory* (New Haven, Conn. and London: Yale University Press, 1963) p. 69.
7. Robert A. Dahl, *Who Governs? Democracy and Power in an American City* (New Haven, Conn.: Yale University Press, 1961) p. 332.
8. To this could be added the case study of 'The Metal Houses' pp. 192–7.
9. Steven Lukes, *Essays in Social Theory* (New York: Columbia University Press, 1977) pp. 13–18.
10. Ibid., p. 18.
11. Stewart Clegg, *The Theory of Power and Organization* (London: Routledge & Kegan Paul, 1979) p. 74.
12. Ibid., p. 99.
13. Ibid., p. 98.
14. Ibid., pp. 99–100.
15. Ibid., p. 95.
16. Ibid., p. 96.
17. Ibid., p. 99.
18. Ibid., p. 97.
19. Ibid., p. 147.
20. Ibid., p. 72 (emphasis in original).
21. Anthony Giddens, *Central Problems in Social Theory: Action, Structure and Contradiction in Social Analysis* (London: Macmillan, 1979) p. 55.
22. Anthony Giddens, *Studies in Social and Political Theory* (London: Hutchinson, 1977) p. 130.
23. Stewart Ranson, Bob Hinings and Royston Greenwood, 'The structuring of organizational structures', *Administrative Science Quarterly*, 25 (1980) pp. 1–17, at p. 2.
24. Ibid., p. 3.
25. Lukes, *Essays in Social Theory*, p. 9.
26. Ibid., p. 10.
27. Ibid., p. 29.
28. The two examples that Lukes presents to illustrate his use of voluntaristic and

deterministic vocabularies are the relationship between Bukharin and Stalin from the mid-1920s to 1938 (pp. 18–21), and the failure of the second British Labour Government of 1929–31 to act in a less orthodox, conservative and ineffective manner (pp. 21–3). These questions are phrased too imprecisely to be offered as subjects for power analysis. Where an outcome is not specified there can be no formulation of relevant counterfactual, and any subsequent discussion is bound to be vague and ill-directed.

29. Lukes, *Essays in Social Theory*, p. 4.
30. Lukes sets out to reject the behavioural emphasis of previous contributors to the community power debate, but, as Alan Bradshaw points out, he returns to 'the individualistic conception that he earlier rejected'. In support of this argument, Bradshaw cites Lukes' claim that to 'see the vocabulary of power in the context of social relationships is to speak of human agents, separately or together, in groups or organizations'. Alan Bradshaw, 'A critique of Steven Lukes' "Power: A Radical View" ', *Sociology*, 10 (1976) pp. 121–7, at p. 125. See also Clegg, *Power and Organization*, pp. 57–64; and Graham Cox, 'Intentions, structures and the dissolution of "power"?', paper presented to the EGOS Symposium on Power, University of Bradford, 6–7 May 1976, p. 5.
31. Lukes, *Essays*, p. 7.
32. Ibid., pp. 7–8.
33. Ibid., p. 13.
34. Ibid., p. 8.
35. Raymond Boudon, *The Uses of Structuralism* (London: Heinemann, 1971) p. 7.
36. Lukes, *Essays*, p. 7.
37. Boudon, *Structuralism*, p. 21. The contrast between these two interpretations is pithily described by George Homans as being between 'what we at least intend to explain . . . [and] . . . what we are prepared simply to take for granted'. George C. Homans, 'What do we mean by social "structure"?', in Peter M. Blau (ed.), *Approaches to the Study of Social Structure* (London: Open Books, 1976) pp. 53–65, at p. 63.
38. S. F. Nadel, *The Theory of Social Structure* (Melbourne: Melbourne University Press, 1957) pp. 150–1.
39. Robert E. Dowse, 'Political socialization', in Dennis Kavanagh and Richard Rose (eds), *New Trends in British Politics* (London and California: Sage, 1977), pp. 221–37, at p. 230.
40. Ibid., p. 230.
41. Nadel, *Theory of Social Structure*, p. 150.
42. Claude Lévi-Strauss, *Structural Anthropology* (New York: Anchor, 1967) p. 271.
43. David Easton, *The Political System* (New York: Knopf, 1953) p. 53.
44. Lukes does not refer to determinism as constituting a fundamental law that the will is everywhere subject to causal law. The emphasis is, rather, that determinism can be regarded as a necessary truth in relation to certain areas of social reality. In other words, an individual's actions may be determined on a given occasion by a particular configuration of standing conditions, events and personalities. Note that such an interpretation does not imply that, given that configuration, the individual affected could never have acted otherwise. It simply means that the costs associated with alternative action appear to have been so high that the 'average person' could not reasonably have been expected to act differently. It is, therefore, predicated on some notion of

average, or standard, behaviour from an actor – rather like Glanville Williams' *Homo juridicus*, 'the ideal man, the moral man, the conscientious man . . . not setting the standard so high that life becomes impossible in ordinary terms'. See note 10 to Chapter 3 above.

45. Karl R. Popper, *The Logic of Scientific Discovery* (London: Hutchinson, 1972) p. 45.

46. Popper, *Logic*, p. 31.

47. James S. Coleman writes that a 'newly developing direction in political science is that of a theory of purposive action', and argues that similar trends can be seen in sociology, psychology and economics. 'Social structure and a Theory of Action', in Blau (ed.) *Approaches to the Study of Social Structure*, p. 78.

48. See pp. 39–40 above.

49. This distinction between the observer's and the subject's levels of meaning is implicit in Weber's functional and action frames of reference. See Max Weber, *The Theory of Social and Economic Organization* (New York: The Free Press, 1964) p. 103. I recognise that the question of whether, and how, an observer can have 'internal understanding' of another's actions is open to dispute. On this see Peter Winch, *The Idea of a Social Science* (London: Routledge & Kegan Paul, 1958) esp. pp. 83–91; and Ernest Gellner, *Cause and Meaning in the Social Sciences* (London: Routledge & Kegan Paul, 1973) Chapter 4, 'The new idealism – cause and meaning in the social sciences'; and I. C. Jarvie, *Concepts and Society* (London: Routledge & Kegan Paul, 1972) Chapter 2, 'Understanding and explaining in the social sciences'. As the brief discussion of 'Intention as essentially problematic' in Chapter 3 above indicates, the view taken here is that even were 'full internal meaning' available to the social scientist, he would not know what to do with it.

50. Robert Merton defines manifest function as 'those objective consequences for a specified unit (person, subgroup, social or cultural system) which contribute to its adjustment or adaptation and were so intended'. Robert K. Merton, *Social Theory and Social Structure* (New York: The Free Press, and London: Collier-Macmillan, 1968) p. 117.

51. Nadel, *Theory of Social Structure*, p. 153.

6. Conclusion

1. Terence Ball, for example, makes the point that the debate has settled very little. 'Power, causation and explanation', *Polity*, 8 (1975–6) pp. 189–214, at p. 198.

2. Steven Lukes, *Power: A Radical View* (London: Macmillan, 1974) p. 34. G. W. Smith points out, though, that Lukes' claims about power 'being "essentially" contestable and "ineradicably" evaluative are overdone'. Must radicals be Marxists? Lukes on power, contestability and alienation', *British Journal of Political Science*, 11 (1981) pp. 405–25, at p. 414.

3. The phrase refers to Bachrach and Baratz and was coined by Richard Merelman, 'On the neo-elitist critique of community power', *American Political Science Review*, 62 (1968) pp. 451–60.

4. S. F. Nadel, *The Theory of Social Structure* (Melbourne: Melbourne University Press, 1957) p. 154.

5. Albert Weale, 'Power inequalities', *Theory and Decision*, 7 (1976) pp. 297–313, at p. 299.

6. Peter Abell, 'The many faces of power and liberty: revealed preference, autonomy and teleological explanation', *Sociology*, 11 (1977) pp. 3–24, at pp. 4–5.

7. Georg Simmel, *The Sociology of Georg Simmel*, trans, ed. and with an intro. by Kurt H. Wolff (New York: The Free Press; and London: Collier-Macmillan, 1950) p. 123.

8. 'Poverty' hovers as a central undefined outcome that preoccupies Hunter yet he does not come to grips with it. That the problem of doing so would be considerable is demonstrated by Peter Townsend, *Poverty in the U.K.* (Harmondsworth: Penguin, 1980).

9. Geraint Parry, *Political Elites* (London: George Allen & Unwin, 1969) p. 118.

10. Robert E. Agger, Daniel Goldrich and Bert E. Swanson, *The Rulers and the Ruled: Political Power and Impotence in American Communities* (New York: Oxford University Press, 1964) pp. 73–8.

Bibliography

Abell, Peter. 'The many faces of power and liberty: revealed preference, autonomy and teleological explanation', *Sociology*, 11 (1977) pp. 3–24.

Agassi, Joseph. 'Methodological individualism', *British Journal of Sociology*, 11 (1960) pp. 244–70.

Agger, Robert E., Goldrich, Daniel and Swanson, Bert E. *The Rulers and the Ruled: Political Power and Impotence in American Communities* (New York: Oxford University Press, 1964).

Allison, Lincoln. 'The nature of the concept of power', *European Journal of Political Research*, 2 (1974) pp. 131–42.

Anscombe, G. E. M. *Intentions* (Oxford: Blackwell, 1957).

Axelrod, Robert. *Conflict of Interest* (Chicago: Markham, 1970).

Azkin, Benjamin. 'On conjecture in political science', *Political Studies*, 14 (1966) pp. 1–14.

Bachrach, Peter. 'A power analysis: the shaping of anti-poverty policy in Baltimore', *Public Policy*, 18 (1970) pp. 155–86.

Bachrach, Peter and Baratz, Morton S. 'The two faces of power', *American Political Science Review*, 56 (1962) pp. 947–52.

——. 'Decisions and nondecisions: an analytic framework', *American Political Science Review*, 57 (1963) pp. 641–51.

——. 'Letter to the editor', *American Political Science Review*, 62 (1968) pp. 1268–9.

——. *Power and Poverty: Theory and Practice* (New York: Oxford University Press, 1970).

——. 'Power and its two faces revisited: a reply to Geoffrey Debnam', *American Political Science Review*, 69 (1975) pp. 900–904.

Ball, Terence. 'Models of power: past and present', *Journal of the History of the Behavioural Sciences*, 11 (1975) pp. 211–22.

——. 'Power, causation and explanation', *Polity*, 8 (1975–6) pp. 189–214.

——. '"Power" revised: a comment on Oppenheim', *Journal of Politics*, 40 (1978) pp. 609–18.

Barry, Brian. 'The economic approach to the analysis of power and conflict', *Government and Opposition*, 9 (1974) pp. 189–223.

——. 'The obscurities of power', *Government and Opposition*, 10 (1975) pp. 250–4.

——. 'Power: an economic analysis', in Brian Barry (ed.), *Power and Political Theory: Some European Perspectives* (London: Wiley, 1976) pp. 67–101.

——. 'Superfox', *Political Studies*, 28 (1980) pp. 136–43.

Barry, Norman P. *Hayek's Social and Economic Philosophy* (London: Macmillan, 1979).

Becquart-Leclercq, Jeanne. 'French mayors and communal policy outputs: the case of small cities', in Roland J. Liebert and Allen W. Imersheim, *Power,*

Paradigms and Community Research (London and California: Sage, 1977) pp. 79–119.

Bell, Colin and Newby, Howard. *Community Studies: An Introduction to the Sociology of the Local Community* (London: George Allen & Unwin, 1971).

Bell, David V. J. *Power, Influence and Authority: An Essay in Political Linguistics* (New York: Oxford University Press, 1975).

Benn, Stanley. 'Power', in Paul Edwards (ed.), *Encyclopedia of Philosophy*, VI (New York: The Free Press, 1967) pp. 424–7.

Bierstedt, Robert. 'An analysis of social power', *American Sociological Review*, 15 (1950) pp. 730–8.

Bilgrami, Akeel. 'Lukes on power and behaviourism', *Inquiry*, 19 (1976) pp. 267–74.

Blais, Andre. 'Power and causality', *Quality and Quantity*, 8 (1974) pp. 45–64.

Blau, Peter M. *Exchange and Power in Social Life* (New York: Wiley, 1964).

Bogart, Leo. 'No opinion, don't know, and maybe no answer', *Public Opinion Quarterly*, 31 (1967) pp. 331–45.

Boudon, Raymond. *The Uses of Structuralism* (London: Heinemann, 1971).

Bradshaw, Alan. 'A critique of Steven Lukes' "Power: a Radical View"', *Sociology*, 10 (1976) pp. 121–7.

Brown, Robert. *Explanation in Social Science* (London: Routledge & Kegan Paul, 1963).

Burns, Tom R. and Buckley, Walter. *Power and Control: Social Structures and their Transformation* (Beverly Hills, Cal.: Sage, 1976).

Burrell, Gibson and Morgan, Gareth. *Sociological Paradigms and Organisational Analysis* (London: Heinemann, 1979).

Butler, David and Stokes, Donald. *Political Change in Britain: The Evolution of Electoral Choice*, 2nd ed. (London: Macmillan, 1974).

Catlin, G. E. C. *The Principles of Politics* (London: George Allen & Unwin, 1930).

Champlin, John R. 'On the study of power', *Politics and Society*, 1 (1970) pp. 91–111.

Chapman, Phillip C. and Scaff, Lawrence A. 'The use and abuse of politics', *Polity*, 8 (1976) pp. 529–57.

Chazel, F. 'Power, cause and force', in Brian Barry (ed.), *Power and Political Theory: Some European Perspectives* (London: Wiley, 1976) pp. 55–65.

Clegg, Stewart. 'Power, theorizing and nihilism', *Theory and Society*, 3 (1976) pp. 65–87.

——. 'Method and sociological discourse', in M. Brenner *et al.* (eds), *The Social Contexts of Method* (London: Croom Helm, 1978) pp. 67–90.

——. *The Theory of Power and Organization* (London: Routledge & Kegan Paul, 1979).

Coleman, James S. 'Social structure and a theory of action', in Peter M. Blau (ed.), *Approaches to the Study of Social Structure* (London: Open Books, 1976) pp. 76–93.

Collingwood, R. G. *The New Leviathan* (Oxford: Clarendon, 1942).

Connolly, William E. *The Terms of Political Discourse* (Lexington, Mass.: Heath, 1974).

Cox, Graham. 'Intentions, structures and the dissolution of "Power"?' Paper presented to the EGOS Symposium on Power, University of Bradford, 6–7 May 1976.

Crenson, Matthew. *The Un-Politics of Air Pollution: A Study of Non-Decisionmaking in the Cities* (Baltimore, Md and London: Johns Hopkins Press, 1971).

Crespigny, Anthony de. 'Power and its forms', *Political Studies*, 16 (1968) pp. 192–205.

Crozier, Michel. 'The problem of power', in Terry Armstrong and Kenneth Cinnamon (eds), *Power and Authority in Law Enforcement* (Springfield, Ill.: Thomas, 1976) pp. 23–38; repr. from *Social Research*, 40 (1973) pp. 211–28.

Curtis, James E. and Petras, John W. 'Community power, power studies and the sociology of knowledge', *Human Organisation*, 29 (1970) pp. 204–18.

Dahl, Robert A. 'The concept of power', *Behavioral Science*, 2 (1957) pp. 201–15.

——. 'A critique of the ruling elite model', *American Political Science Review*, 52 (1958) pp. 463–9.

——. *Who Governs? Democracy and Power in an American City* (New Haven, Conn. and London: Yale University Press, 1961).

——. 'Power', in David L. Sills (ed.), *International Encyclopedia of the Social Sciences* (New York: Macmillan and The Free Press, 1968) vol. XII, pp. 405–15.

——. *Modern Political Analysis*, 2nd ed. (Englewood, N.J.: Prentice Hall, 1970).

D'Antonio, William V., Ehrlich, Howard J. and Erickson, Eugene C. 'Further notes on the study of community power', *American Sociological Review*, 27 (1962) pp. 848–54.

Debnam, Geoffrey R. 'Nondecisions and power: the two faces of Bachrach and Baratz', *American Political Science Review*, 69 (1975) pp. 889–99.

——. 'Rejoinder to "Comment" by Peter Bachrach and Morton S. Baratz', *American Political Science Review*, 69 (1975) pp. 905–7.

Dobriner, William M. *Social Structures and Systems: A Sociological Overview* (Santa Monica, Cal.: Goodyear, 1969).

Domhoff, G. William. *Who Really Rules? New Haven and Community Power Reexamined* (Santa Monica, Cal.: Goodyear, 1978).

Dowse, Robert E. 'Political socialization', in Dennis Kavanagh and Richard Rose (eds), *New Trends in British Politics* (London and California: Sage, 1977) pp. 221–37.

Dror, Yehezkel. *Public Policymaking Reexamined* (Scranton, Penn.: Chandler, 1968).

Dunleavy, Patrick. 'An issue centred approach to the study of power', *Political Studies*, 24 (1976) pp. 423–34.

Easton, David. *The Political System* (New York: Knopf, 1953).

Ehrlich, Howard J. 'The social psychology of reputations for community leadership', *The Sociological Quarterly*, 8 (1967) pp. 514–30.

Elster, Jon. 'Some conceptual problems in political theory', in Brian Barry (ed.), *Power and Political Theory: Some European Perspectives* (London: Wiley, 1976) pp. 245–70.

——. *Logic and Society: Contradictions and Possible Worlds* (Chichester: Wiley, 1978).

——. 'The treatment of counterfactuals: reply to Brian Barry', *Political Studies*, 28 (1980) pp. 144–7.

——. 'Reply to comments', *Inquiry*, 23 (1980) pp. 213–32.

Emmett, Dorothy. 'The concept of power', *Proceedings of the Aristotelian Society*, new series 54, (1953–4) pp. 1–26.

Follett, Mary Parker. *Dynamic Administration* (London: Management Publications Trust Ltd, 1934).

Fox, Alan. *Beyond Contract* (London: Faber, 1974).

Frankenberg, Ronald. *Communities in Britain: Social Life in Town and Country* (Harmondsworth: Penguin, 1966).

Frey, Frederick W. 'Comment: on issues and nonissues in the study of power', *American Political Science Review*, 65 (1971) pp. 1081–1101.

Friedrich, Carl J. *Constitutional Government and Democracy: Theory and Practice in Europe and America* (Boston, Mass.: Ginn, 1946).

Frohock, Frederick. *The Nature of Political Inquiry* (Homewood, Ill.: Dorsey, 1967).

——. 'The structure of "Politics"', *American Political Science Review*, 72 (1978) pp. 859–70.

Garrard, John A. 'The history of local political power – some suggestions for analysis', *Political Studies*, 25 (1977) pp. 252–69.

Gaventa, John. *Power and Powerlessness: Quiescence and Rebellion in an Appalachian Valley* (Oxford: Clarendon, 1980).

Gellner, Ernest. *Cause and meaning in the social sciences* (London: Routledge & Kegan Paul, 1973).

Georgiou, Petro. 'The concept of power: a critique and an alternative', *Australian Journal of Politics and History*, 23 (1977) pp. 252–67.

Gerth, H. H. and Wright Mills, C. (eds). *From Max Weber: Essays in Sociology* (New York: Oxford University Press, 1958).

Ghosh, S. C. 'Decision, process and power: a conceptual approach', *Indian Journal of Political Science*, 36 (1975) pp. 344–57.

Gibson, Quentin. 'Power', *Philosophy of the Social Sciences*, 1 (1971) pp. 101–12.

Giddens, Anthony. ' "Power" in the recent writings of Talcott Parsons', *Sociology*, 2 (1968) pp. 257–72.

——. *New Rules of Sociological Method* (London: Hutchinson, 1976).

——. *Studies in Social and Political Theory* (London: Hutchinson, 1977).

——. *Central Problems in Social Theory: Action, Structure and Contradiction in Social Analysis* (London: Macmillan, 1979).

Gilbert, Claire W. 'Communities, power structures and research bias', *Polity*, 4 (1971) pp. 218–35.

Goldman, Alvin I. 'Toward a theory of social power', *Philosophical Studies*, 23 (1972) pp. 221–68.

Greer, Edward. 'Air pollution and corporate power: municipal reform limits in a black city', *Politics and Society*, 4 (1974) pp. 483–510.

Hall, Edward T. *Beyond Culture* (New York: Anchor, 1976).

Hammack, David C. 'Problems in the historical study of power in the cities and towns of the United States, 1800–1960', *American Historical Review*, 83 (1978) pp. 323–49.

Hampshire, Stuart. *Thought and Action* (London: Chatto & Windus, 1959).

Hart, H. L. A. *Punishment and Responsibility: Essays in the Philosophy of Law* (Oxford: Clarendon Press, 1968).

Hayek, F. A. *Studies in Philosophy, Politics and Economics* (London: Routledge & Kegan Paul, 1967).

Hindess, Barry. 'On three dimensional power', *Political Studies*, 24 (1976) pp. 329–33.

Homans, George C. *The Human Group* (London: Routledge & Kegan Paul, 1951).

——. 'What do we mean by "social structure"?', in Peter M. Blau (ed.), *Approaches to the Study of Social Structure* (London: Open Books, 1976) pp. 53–65.

Hunter, Floyd. *Community Power Structure: A Study of Decision Makers* (New York: Anchor, 1963).

———. *Community Power Succession: Atlanta's Policy-Makers Revisited* (Chapel Hill, N.C.: University of North Carolina, 1980).

Jarvie, I. C. *Concepts and Society* (London: Routledge & Kegan Paul, 1972).

———. *Universities and Left Review*, 2 (1958–9) p. 57.

Jessop, Bob. 'On the commensurability of power and structural constraint'. Paper presented to the EGOS Symposium on Power, University of Bradford, 6–7 May 1976.

Jones, Allan. 'Power politics', in David V. Edwards, *International Political Analysis: Readings* (New York: Holt, Rinehart and Winston, 1970) pp. 207–25.

Jones, G. W. *Responsibility and Government* (London: London School of Economics, 1977).

Kadushin, C. 'Power, influence and social circles: a new methodology for studying opinion makers', *American Sociological Review*, 33 (1968) pp. 685–99.

Kornberg, Allen and Perry, Simon D. 'Conceptual models of power and their applicability to empirical research in politics', *Political Science*, 18 (1966) pp. 52–70.

Kuhn, Alfred. *The Study of Society: A Unified Approach* (Homewood, Ill.: Irwin, 1963).

Lane, Jan-Erik, 'On the use of the word "political" ', in Brian Barry (ed.), *Power and Political Theory: Some European Perspectives* (London: Wiley, 1976).

Lasswell, Harold D. and Kaplan, Abraham. *Power and Society* (New Haven, Conn.: Yale University Press, 1950).

Lévi-Strauss, Claude. *Structural Anthropology* (New York: Anchor, 1967).

Levy, Frank, Meltsner, Arnold J. and Wildavsky, Aaron. *Urban Outcomes: Schools, Streets and Libraries* (Berkeley, Cal.: University of California Press, 1974).

Locke, John. *The Second Treatise of Civil Government and A Letter Concerning Toleration*, ed. with an Introduction by J. W. Gough (Oxford: Blackwell, 1948).

Lockwood, David. 'Some remarks on "The Social System" ', *British Journal of Sociology*, 7 (1956) pp. 134–43.

Lukes, Steven. *Power: A Radical View* (London: Macmillan, 1974).

———. 'Reply to Bradshaw', *Sociology*, 10 (1976) pp. 129–32.

———. *Essays in Social Theory* (New York: Columbia University Press, 1977).

MacIntyre, Alasdair. 'A mistake about causality in social science', in *Philosophy, Politics and Society*, 2nd series, Peter Laslett and W. G. Runciman (eds.) (Oxford: Blackwell, 1969) pp. 48–70.

McLachlan, Hugh V. 'Is "power" an evaluative concept?', *British Journal of Sociology*, 32 (1981) pp. 392–410.

Maguire, John. 'Power', *Cambridge Review*, 96 (1975) pp. 116–18.

March, James G. 'The power of power', in David Easton (ed.), *Varieties of Political Theory* (Englewood Cliffs, N.J.: Prentice-Hall, 1966) pp. 30–70.

May, R. *Power and Innocence: A Search for the Sources of Violence* (London: Souvenir, 1974).

Mayer, Adrian C. 'Quasi-groups in the study of complex societies' in Michael Banton (ed.), *The Social Anthropology of Complex Societies* (London: Tavistock, 1966) pp. 97–122.

Meiland, John. 'Unintentional actions', *Philosophical Review*, 72 (1963) pp. 377–81:

Merelman, Richard. 'On the neo-elitist critique of community power', *American Political Science Review*, 62 (1968) pp. 451–60.

———. 'Reply to "Comment" by Bachrach and Baratz', *American Political Science Review*, 62 (1968) pp. 1269.

Merton, Robert K. 'The role set', in Peter Worsley (ed.), *Modern Sociology: Introductory Readings*, 2nd ed. (Harmondsworth: Penguin, 1978) pp. 341–51; repr. from Robert K. Merton, 'The role-set: problems in sociological theory', *British Journal of Sociology*, 8 (1957) pp. 110–20.

———. *Social Theory and Social Structure* (New York: The Free Press, 1968).

———. 'The unanticipated consequences of social action', in Robert K. Merton, *Sociological Ambivalence and Other Essays* (New York: The Free Press, 1976) pp. 145–55.

Midgaard, Knut. 'Cooperative negotiations and bargaining: some notes on power and powerlessness', in Brian Barry (ed.), *Power and Political Theory: Some European Perspectives* (London: Wiley, 1976) pp. 117–37.

Mill, John Stuart. *Utilitarianism, Liberty and Representative Government* (London: Dent, 1910).

Mokken, R. J. and Stokman F. N. 'Power and influence as political phenomena', in Brian Barry (ed.), *Power and Political Theory: Some European Perspectives* (London: Wiley, 1976) pp. 33–54.

Morgenthau, Hans J. *Scientific Man vs Power Politics* (Chicago: University of Chicago Press, 1965).

Morriss, Peter. 'The essentially uncontestable concepts of power', in Michael Freeman and David Robertson (eds), *The Frontiers of Political Theory: Essays in a Revitalized Discipline* (Brighton: Harvester, 1980) pp. 198–232.

Nadel, S. F. *The Theory of Social Structure* (Melbourne: Melbourne University Press, 1957).

Nagel, Jack H. *The Descriptive Analysis of Power* (New Haven, Conn. and London: Yale University Press, 1975).

Newton, Kenneth. 'Democracy, community power and decision-making', *Political Studies*, 20 (1972) pp. 484–7.

Ng, Sik Hung. *The Social Psychology of Power* (London: Academic Press, 1980).

Nicholson, Peter. 'What is politics: determining the scope of political science', *Il Politico*, 42 (1977) pp. 228–49.

Oppenheim, Felix E. ' "Power" revisited', *Journal of Politics*, 40 (1978) pp. 589–608.

———. ' "Power"; one more visit: a response to Terence Ball', *Journal of Politics*, 40 (1978) pp. 619–21.

Parenti, Michael. *Power and the Powerless* (New York: St Martin's Press, 1978).

Parry, Geraint. *Political Elites* (London: George Allen & Unwin, 1969).

——— and Peter Morriss, 'When is a decision not a decision?', in Ivor Crewe (ed.), *British Political Sociology Yearbook*, vol. I (London: Croom Helm, 1974) pp. 317–36.

Parsons, Talcott. *Structure and Process in Modern Society* (New York: The Free Press, 1960).

Partridge, P. H. 'Some notes on the concept of power', *Political Studies*, 11 (1963) pp. 107–25.

Polsby, Nelson W. *Community Power and Political Theory* (New Haven, Conn. and London: Yale University Press, 1963). Second edition, sub-titled *A Further Look at Problems of Evidence and Inference*, published 1980.

——. 'Community power meets air pollution', *Contemporary Sociology*, 1 (1972) pp. 99–101.

——. 'Empirical investigation of mobilization of bias in community power research', *Political Studies*, 27 (1979) pp. 527–41.

——. 'Rejoinder to Newton', *Political Studies*, 27 (1979) pp. 548–9.

Popper, K. R. *The Open Society and its Enemies*, vol. II (London: Routledge & Kegan Paul, 1966).

——. *The Logic of Scientific Discovery* (London: Hutchinson, 1972).

Presthus, Robert. *Men at the Top* (New York: Oxford University Press, 1964).

Ranson, Stewart, Hinings, Bob and Greenwood, Royston. 'The structuring of organizational structures', *Administrative Science Quarterly*, 25 (1980) pp. 1–17.

Riker, William H. 'Some ambiguities in the notion of power', *American Political Science Review*, 58 (1964) pp. 341–9.

Rogow, Arnold A. and Lasswell, Harold D. *Power, Corruption and Rectitude* (Westport, Conn.: Greenwood, 1963).

Rose, Arnold M. *The Power Structure: Political Processes in American Society* (New York: Oxford University Press, 1967).

Runciman, W. G. *Social Science and Political Theory*, 2nd ed. (Cambridge: Cambridge University Press, 1969).

Russell, Bertrand. *Power: A New Social Analysis* (London: George Allen & Unwin, 1938).

Schattschneider, E. E. *The Semi-Sovereign People: A Realist's View of Democracy in America* (New York: Holt, Rinehart & Winston, 1960).

Schick, Allen. 'Systems politics and systems budgeting', *Public Administration Review*, 29 (1969) pp. 137–51.

Simmel, Georg. 'The dyad and the triad' in Lewis A. Coser and Bernard Rosenberg, *Sociological Theory: A Book of Readings* (New York: Macmillan, 1957) pp. 66–76. Repr. from *The Sociology of Georg Simmel*. transl. with an Introduction by Kurt H. Wolff (Glencoe, Ill: The Free Press, 1950) pp. 122–5, 145–53.

Simon, Herbert. 'Notes on the observation and measurement of power', *Journal of Politics*, 15 (1953) pp. 500–516.

——. *Models of Man, Social and Rational* (New York: Wiley, 1957).

Smith, T. V. 'Power: its ubiquity and legitimacy', *American Political Science Review*, 45 (1951) pp. 693–702.

Snyder, Richard C. 'A decision-making approach to the study of political phenomena', in Roland Young (ed.), *Approaches to the Study of Politics* (Evanston, Ill.: Northwestern University Press, 1958) pp. 3–38.

Stoljar, S. J. *Groups and Entities: An Inquiry into Corporate Theory* (Canberra: Australian National University Press, 1973).

Tawney, R. H. *Equality* (London: George Allen & Unwin, 1931).

Thompson, Kirk. 'Constitutional theory and political action', *Journal of Politics*, 31 (1969) pp. 655–81.

Townsend, Peter. *Poverty in the U.K.* (Harmondsworth: Penguin, 1980).

Van Doorn, J. A. A. 'Sociology and the problem of power', *Sociologia Neerlandica*, 1 (1962–3) pp. 3–51.

Walliman, Isidor, Tatsis, Nicholas and Zito, George. 'On Max Weber's definition of power', *Australian and New Zealand Journal of Sociology*, 13 (1977) pp. 231–5.

Weale, Albert. 'Power inequalities', *Theory and Decision*, 7 (1976) pp. 297–313.

Weber, Max. *The Theory of Social and Economic Organization*, translated by A. M.

Henderson and Talcott Parsons, and edited and introduced by Talcott Parsons (New York: The Free Press, 1964).

White, D. M. 'Power and intentions', *American Political Science Review*, 65 (1971) pp. 749–59.

——. 'The problem of power', *British Journal of Political Science*, 2 (1972) pp. 479–90.

——. *The Concept of Power* (Morristown, N.J.: General Learning Press, 1976).

——. 'The concept of power: semantic chaos or underlying consensus'. Paper prepared for delivery at the Moscow IPSA Congress, 12–18 August 1979.

Williams, Glanville. *Textbook of Criminal Law* (London: Stevens, 1978).

Winch, Peter. *The Idea of a Social Science*. (London: Routledge & Kegan Paul, 1958).

Wisdom, J. O. 'Situational individualism and the emergent group properties', in Robert Borger and Frank Cioffi, *Explanation in the Behavioural Sciences* (London: Cambridge University Press, 1970) pp. 271–96.

Wittman, Donald. 'Various concepts of power: equivalence among ostensibly unrelated approaches', *British Journal of Political Science*, 6 (1976) pp. 449–62.

Wolfinger, Raymond E. 'Reputation and reality in the study of community power', *American Sociological Review*, 25 (1960) pp. 636–44.

——. 'A plea for a decent burial', *American Sociological Review*, 27 (1962) pp. 841–7.

——. 'Nondecisions and the study of local politics', *American Political Science Review*, 65 (1971) pp. 1063–80.

——. 'Rejoinder to Frey's "Comment"', *American Political Science Review*, 65 (1971) pp. 1102–4.

Wrong, Dennis H. *Skeptical Sociology* (London: Heinemann, 1977).

——. *Power: Its Forms, Bases and Uses* (Oxford: Blackwell, 1979).

Young, R. A. 'Steven Lukes's radical view of power', *Canadian Journal of Political Science*, 11 (1978) pp. 639–49.

Index